D0854306

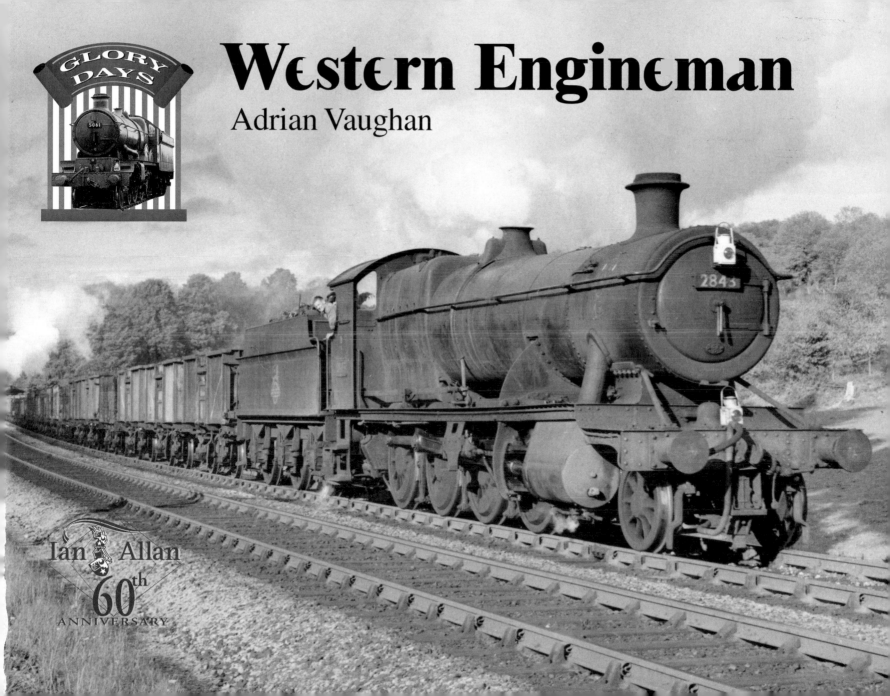

GLORY DAYS

Western Engineman

Adrian Vaughan

Ian Allan
60th
ANNIVERSARY

Front cover:
No 7006 *Lydford Castle* brought the 7am Swindon–Penzance into Newton Abbot. No 4098 *Kidwelly Castle* then 'came on the front' to assist over the banks to Plymouth, on 19 July 1958. *R. C. Riley*

Back cover:
No 5058 *Earl St. Aldwyn* leaves Teignmouth with the up 'Devonian' on 1 July 1957. *R. C. Riley*

Title page:
Drama on Dainton. No 2843, assisted by the '51xx' class 'banker', heaves about 20 wagons of coal up the 1-in-36 section of Dainton Bank. The train consists of about 15 16-tonners, three wooden 12-tonners and two 20-ton 'Loco Coal' wagons. This makes the load equal to 27 loaded 10-ton coal wagons. In 1936, the maximum permitted load for a '28xx' class engine unassisted on Dainton was 20 loaded 10-tonners or about 340 tons. The driver and fireman are looking out cheerfully, as well they might: the fireman has the fire right and the driver's-side injector can be seen to be running (so probably both injectors are on), but in spite of that, and in spite of full regulator and a long cut-off as evidenced by the position of the reversing rod, the boiler is at full pressure, a steady roar of steam accompanying the 'four beats to the bar' gunshot exhaust from the chimney. A familiar scene to Bob in 1937, the same engines and (probably) the same men are at work on 17 May 1957.
courtesy Hugh Ballantyne

Opposite:
No 4704 stands quietly at Newton Abbot after bringing in an express from Paddington – almost 194 miles.
Adrian Vaughan collection

Contents

First published 2002

ISBN 0 7110 2882 6

All rights reserved. No part of this book may be reproduced or transmitted in any form or by any means, electronic or mechanical, including photocopying, recording or by any information storage and retrieval system, without permission from the Publisher in writing.

© Adrian Vaughan 2002

Published by Ian Allan Publishing

an imprint of Ian Allan Publishing Ltd, Hersham, Surrey KT12 4RG.

Printed by Ian Allan Printing Ltd, Hersham, Surrey KT12 4RG.

Code: 0205/B1

Author's Preface

I met Robert Nicks by chance in 1978. We talked and he promised to send me a written account of his life. This he did — 15,000 hand-written words on foolscap. In moving house I mislaid his manuscript, which did not come to light again until 2000. A good time to remember a better-organised railway. Energetic as ever, Bob had tumbled his memories onto the pages, resulting in a rather colloquial grammar and a jumbled sequence of events. My job was that of editor: putting events into chronological order, re-writing sparingly, only where it was essential to improve clarity, and adding some little commentary on what he had written. The words in this book are as far as possible as Bob wrote them to me; the usages of the Devonshire dialect and the footplate language are scattered about.

In order not to sanitise or falsify history, I have included Bob's references to drinking beer or cider whilst at work. 'Wetting the whistle' on the footplate of shunting engines, branch goods trains and pottering local goods trains was a fact of life for some steam engine drivers. When these same men moved into the warm, upholstered cab of a diesel, they drank no more beer or cider on duty because the dangers were obvious and real. Bob had his share of cider on lowly jobs. He was also a highly conscientious, skilled and committed railwayman.

Acknowledgements

I should like to thank Mrs Ivy Nicks, her daughter Ann and her son Michael for their kind assistance in preparing this book. Thanks too to Ann and her husband Terry Hall for their hospitality.

My thanks are due to photographers Hugh Ballantyne, Sid Nash and Russell Mulford for their generosity, and Larry Crosier to Mr R. C. Riley, for his kind assistance with searching out the relevant slides and supplying caption information, and to David Collins, Larry Crosier, John Morris and Peter Jordan, all of whom supplied additional information.

I should also like to acknowledge the devotion of former Newton Abbot locomen Arthur King and Ron Sharland, both of whom fired to Bob Nicks (they are two of only 12 men surviving from the gang that entered GWR service at Newton Abbot in 1937-9), and of Felicity Cole, Curator of the Newton Abbot Town & GWR Museum, through her enthusiastic help in opening the museum specially for me on her day off and supplying me with unique images.

Thanks too go to Driver Colin Pulleyblank, who started at Newton Abbot shed in 1937, for thoughtfully donating the portable immersion heater to the museum.

Introduction

Robert Nicks was born into a railway family. His grandfather had been Ganger of the Christow length of the Teign Valley branch until he was demoted after too close an acquaintance with a flagon of cider. His father was on the gang at Christow. When Robert's father was promoted to Ganger of the Dawlish Warren length, in about 1928, the family moved to Kenton, near Starcross.

Robert Nicks was born here at Doddiscombsleigh.

Robert was a very intelligent and extremely energetic countryman. He was, perhaps, a little shy and sensitive as a teenager, and from this he developed into a very caring adult.

Bob wanted to be an engineer. His mother encouraged him and he attended Exeter technical college, but his parents could not afford to buy him an apprenticeship and so he went into the engine sheds at Exeter.

It was in Kenton that Bob met his future wife, Ivy. They were 'going together' from the age of 15. Both of them worked six days a week, on Sundays they sang together in Kenton church choir. Ivy was born 24 November 1914. Her father had served in the Devonshire Regiment during the Great War, and when he was demobbed he came home to unemployment until he found work on a Devon County Council road-maintenance gang. After he retired he got a job as a gardener at Lesley House in Kenton. Ivy left school aged 15 and worked as a parlour maid in Lesley House. She was an intelligent, energetic, devoted, caring wife and mother and daughter, and cared for her mother until she died, aged 89, in 1980. Her father continued to work daily in the gardens of Lesley House. He generally looked after himself, but Ivy visited him him daily, baking him cakes and doing his laundry. He died, still working, aged 96. Ivy is still with us, a calm and dignified lady.

Ivy and Bob were married in Kenton parish church on 3 July 1937. Ivy has told me that they had a honeymoon week in Ashford, Kent, courtesy of a cousin, and took a day trip to Boulogne. In 1938, with a cheap mortgage advanced by Bob's trade union — the Associated Society of Locomotive Enginemen & Firemen (ASLEF) — they bought a brand-new bungalow in Lyndhurst Avenue, Kingskerswell. Bob sold his bachelor's motorcycle and bought a push-bike on which he cycled to work at all hours of the day and night. In the freezing snowy winters which came most years in those days, he went on foot. Ivy always had his food ready on time. He was never late for work — and he never passed a signal at 'Danger', either.

Bob's energy and good nature was prodigious. If a neighbour in Kingskerswell was ill, Bob would do his or her chores, plant their potatoes if necessary, do their shopping. One very sick, 80-year-old widow, he 'adopted' and cared for her as he would his mother. He was an instructor at Newton Abbot Mutual Improvement Class, teaching the young ones the Rules and Regulations and the working of locomotives. He was for many years Secretary of the ASLEF at Newton Abbot. In his surviving papers are the rule books for the railway pension funds which he studied and understood so that he could answer the questions of his comrades and give advice. At home he maintained a flower garden at the front of the house and a vegetable garden at the back, and grew more food on an allotment.

Ivy and Bob found time, between his shifts and his voluntary work, to go out together with the children, Michael and Ann. Ivy recalled a Sunday in 1942 when she and Bob and little Ann were in Torquay together. A German raider roared in, dropped bombs and strafed the people on the seafront and beach. An hotel received a direct hit, and, as everyone else dived for cover, Bob was still standing up observing the carnage. Soon he was covered in feathers as the filling of all the pillows and mattresses of the hotel came wafting back to earth. A bomb landed on St Mary's church, killing many of the members of the Sunday school class inside.

Ivy supported Bob devotedly in his railway career. And indeed, so did thousands of other wives, as Ivy, modest as ever, was quick to point out. She helped him to learn the Rule Book and examined him on 'The Locomotive: Its Faults and Remedies', reading the relevant book and cleverly asking questions. If he was due out of the house at 3am she was ahead of him, his breakfast prepared and his food for two days away from home, packed. He had to carry with him all necessary food for a 'double home' trip — two days away, at work. There would be sandwiches for each day's journey and food to make a hot meal or meals at the lodging at the far end of the journey. This was because food was only obtainable with a ration book issued to each family — the landlady at the lodge would have no food for her enginemen lodgers. No extra food ration was allowed to men working as locomotive firemen but having an allotment and some chickens provided some extra food while, in the country there was always the chance of a little extra beef or bacon from illicitly slaughtered animals.

Sometimes Ivy packed raw rashers of bacon and fresh eggs to be cooked by the landlady of Bob's lodge at the far end of the journey, sometimes she cooked beef and vegetables, packed them in a china

Robert and Ivy at the doorway of Kenton parish church on their wedding day, 3 July 1937. The bridesmaid is Bob's cousin, Betty.
courtesy Ivy Nicks

bowl, with a cover tied over it. The preparation, every other day, of such large amounts of food, in addition to preparing meals for her family at home was, clearly, an almighty burden for her and all the other footplatemen's wives. Ivy accepted the challenge and rose to it magnificently. Since the railways were vital to the war effort then the wives were even more basically vital to that effort.

Bob and Ivy were a devoted couple and both were devoted to 'The Job' — the railway, the civilised, steam-hauled railway. Cutting costs actually costs us efficiency and something more: quite priceless humanity.

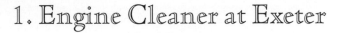

1. Engine Cleaner at Exeter

I was born in Doddiscombsleigh in Devon. My father was in the track gang based at Christow, on the Teign Valley line of the GWR. One of his best friends was Spencer Lee, who was then driving on the branch trains. Spencer had known me since I was a babe in long clothes. As a boy I used to meet him on Christow station and get on his engine for a ride for the two miles or so to Ashton. My father was appointed ganger of the Dawlish Warren length, and we moved from Christow to Kenton, a mile or so the Exeter side of Starcross. I grew up with the railway, and my mother encouraged me in the idea of becoming an engineer and working for the Great Western Railway.

At the beginning of July 1928, three weeks from my 14th birthday and not long before I was due to leave school, my parents obtained letters of good character for me from a local clergyman and my schoolmaster and then applied to the Newton Abbot Locomotive Superintendent, Mr Christison,

for an interview. My mother went with me on the appointed day. She asked if I could be apprenticed as a loco fitter. He said I could but she would have to pay the company a fee of £100 — which, of course, she didn't have, and, even if she had been able to find the money, there was no guarantee that there would be a position for me on the GWR after I'd finished my apprenticeship. The Superintendent could see I was really disappointed and said: 'I could put your name down on the list for the next vacancy for an engine cleaner, and you then could become an engine driver one day.' That is how it was in those days — three million unemployed, and people were queuing for an engine cleaner's job. My mother and I went home, having achieved the entry of my name on a list of aspiring engine cleaners.

I left school at the end of the summer term, working in little jobs for 10 months and going to Exeter Tech for evening classes. Then, in April 1929, I got a letter from Mr Christison to report to Exeter St David's

I understand that R.M. Hicks has been selected for appointment on G.W.R. — I have great pleasure in stating that I have known him all his life — and I then him to be a thoroughly reliable, straight-forward and <u>truthful</u> lad - one

who can be trusted to carry out his duties to the best of his ability — He comes of a most respectable family - who have lived in Doddiscombsleigh (on his mothers side) for some generations. and who are very highly esteemed — I quite expect to hear

that R.M. Hicks is giving every satisfaction.

I.J. Buckingham
J.P.
late Rector of Doddiscombsleigh & Prebendary of Exeter.

June 29th 1929.

station to have an oral and eyesight exam. When I got to the Chief Clerk's office I found that there were two jobs going and 52 other chaps assembled. Four of these would be chosen to go to Swindon for further examination. I looked at the others, many of whom were aged 18 or older; they seemed like men beside my 14 years and I thought I had no chance, but I was one of the lucky four to be selected to go to Swindon. I had another oral and eyesight exam on arriving. I had to lodge a night there. The next day we went to Park House for a medical exam under Dr Swinhoe, who did not miss much.

Finally, in May 1929, I had a letter from Mr Christison informing me that I had been accepted as a cleaner for Exeter St David's shed, to start at 6am on 1 July 1929 — three weeks before my 15th birthday.

Once I had it confirmed that I had a job in the sheds I bought a brand-new BSA three-speed cycle — which I still have. I couldn't lodge in Exeter on 4/- (20p) a day — it would have been a skinflint existence. That first morning I rose at quarter past four, left home at five and cycled to St David's — about 8 miles. I got to Exeter shed 10 minutes before time and waited outside the foreman's office. I had to wait for the day foreman, Mr Seward, to finish his discussion with the night foreman (who then went home) and call me in. I was asked a few details about my family and where I lived and was then taken to the timekeeper's office, where I was booked on as the junior hand and given check No 236. I was a *junior* boy, not even a boy cleaner.

My work was to be general dogsbody on the shed: call boy, messenger for the timekeeper and Chief Clerk, office cleaner. I was a proper boy, and felt rather afraid and timid to be working with so many total strangers. My work as call boy entailed knowledge of where all the shed staff and loco crews lived. I wrote them all into a pocket book which still have and I can go back over the names of some wonderful men.

As call boy my duties were in the office, in the timekeeper's office answering the telephones and in the stores with the storeman. I had my meals in the stores and kept my cycle there. I was rather short and could not put the phone to my ear, so the Chief Clerk got a block of wood for me to stand on. Tom Andrews had to go with me round Exeter, Top Town and St Thomas to show me where all the streets were where the staff lived. I had two turns — days and nights, 8.30am and 10pm, —

starting on nights. I worked in the knee-length trousers I had worn at school until the end of the summer workings 1929.

I had to clean the foreman's office daily as well as having to take out call papers to drivers and firemen at their homes when their turns of duty were altered. I fetched all letters for the shed foreman from the Superintendent's office and took letters from the shed to the letter sorter's office on the down platform at St David's, and also took letters to the letter office and to the trains.

Letters for Newton Abbot were given to the guard of the 9.26am to Kingswear, worked by Exeter men. One driver on this job was my friend Spencer Lee. He let me have rides on whatever engine he was driving; I recall 4012 *Knight of the Thistle*, 4015 *Knight of St.John*, 4045 *Prince John* and 4049 *Princess Maud*, but there were many others. As I got better known, other drivers would let me start their engines from the shed signal and take them onto the main line. This made up for the hard and mundane side of work. Once a week when on the day turn, I had to clean all

Exeter shed yard in 1913. Saddle tank No 1956 has some elbow grease applied by a boy cleaner.
Adrian Vaughan collection

the windows of the offices and cabins and help the storeman unload the stores truck bringing the spares, lubricating oil and cotton waste ordered from Swindon. There was also a truck of firelighters to be unloaded once a month. (These were made in prisons: sticks of wood, nailed together in hollow squares to be thrown into the fireboxes, lit and the coal piled around them.)

I also helped the shed toolman, who was responsible for each set of engine tools at Exeter, including all the batteries that were used on the engines for the Automatic Train Control (ATC). A truck of these would arrive on a train and be brought to us by an engine coming to shed. I helped to unload the new batteries and load in the old. I helped the storeman refill the shed oil supply which the drivers used daily when they prepared an engine. The oil was transferred from barrels into the main tank using an engine's brake ejector to create a vacuum. I had the job of stoking the engine used to supply the steam for this and for tube cleaning or boiler washing so that was a good beginning for me as I was in charge of an engine's boiler and fire, admittedly a stationary one. One of the day's last jobs was to trim the stop block lamp at the west end of the yard so there was always a bright red light.

At the end of my first week I was approached to join a trade union, either the NUR or ASLEF. I gave it my consideration, and, as my father was in the NUR and had been for 30 years and there was some doubt about my keeping the job after the summer service (and also the NUR

subscription was less, and when you are on four bob a day you have to consider the coppers) I decided on the NUR.

My second week on shift started at midnight on Saturday/Sunday, and I left home around 11pm. On arriving at the shed, Cleaner Andrews showed me how to fill in the call sheet, because there were a lot of men to be called between midnight and 6am. We were under a senior caller-up, Jack Hooper, a shedman who was permanently on nights. Our greatest number of drivers and firemen for calling lived in the St Thomas and Exwick areas, and the districts had to be divided between call boys. Immediately on starting on Sunday you had to make out your call sheet and be off out; you would come back in and grab just enough time for a meal break and drink and then be off out again — it was a hard job on a dark night in the wind and the rain. I would get back into the shed about 6.30am. We boys would try to keep out of the way for the last two hours, sign off-duty and cycle home — after cycling miles around St Thomas and Exwick.

On Monday mornings, after a night out calling-up, it was my inescapable task to wash out the timekeeper's office, make his fire, dust and polish his table, and then wash the floors in the enginemen's cabins and scrub their food tables until I booked off at 9am to cycle home.

That first night shift over, I felt so tired and weary even before cycling 8 miles home. I arrived about 10am with mother looking out down the road for me. Her first words were: 'How have you got on?' 'All right,' I said, 'but I ain't half tired.' I fell into a chair and she started frying me a breakfast. I was fast asleep by the time she'd got the bacon in the pan but she woke me and I enjoyed my meal. I then had a good wash and went to bed about 11am and heard nothing until my mother came up and called me at 8pm. I was still tired but she gave me a good meal and at 9pm I was back on the road on my cycle.

This time I was booked on only till 7am. When I got to work it was cleaning the offices and scrubbing floors. The timekeeper's office floor was hardwood blocks, and that was scrubbed white like a butcher's block; if it wasn't up to the mark, 'Coaxer' Gill, the clerk, would be on your tail. I fetched coal for office fires and for the cabin fires. Then I went out calling-up.

After I had been at work for a year I was entitled to a privilege season ticket, and I could cycle into Starcross and

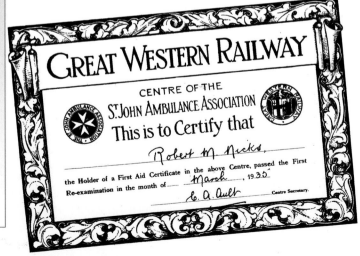

GREAT WESTERN RAILWAY

CENTRE OF THE

St. John Ambulance Association

This is to Certify that

Robert M. Nicks,

the Holder of a First Aid Certificate in the above Centre, passed the First Re-examination in the month of ...... March ......, 19.30.

E. A. Ault   Centre Secretary.

go to work by train. I only had to cycle to Exeter when I was on nights, Sundays and cycle home coming off nights of a Saturday. I was by now well known to all the Exeter drivers and firemen and several from Newton Abbot, and I often rode home on the footplate from Exeter to Starcross on the 6.50pm stopping train which Exeter men worked to Plymouth. The Exeter shed foreman, then a Mr Russell, would let me put my check in a few minutes before time so I could catch this train home. Provided you worked hard Mr Russell would see you were all right with things like that.

Driver Frank Richards and his fireman Bill Prout liked to see how anyone would shape up firing, and they got me firing from Exeter to Starcross. I made a good job of it, so Frank told me to put down the water scoop when we went over Exminster troughs. We were sailing along nicely and I put the scoop down, but I couldn't get it back up; when we got to the far end the tender overflowed and we were nearly washed overboard. The pair just smiled and said I could do it as well as any of the others that tried. But by the end of the week I had the knack and could do it a treat.

During 1934 I studied for my First Aider's Certificate with the St John's Ambulance Brigade. I passed the exam and kept up my skills in that department for the rest of my career.

I was the first cleaner to be taken on at Exeter since May 1926, so there was a lot of difference in seniority between me and the earlier intake. There were also still some men working as cleaners who had been taken on in May 1924. They were earning 7/- (35p) a day and they had got married on that — at least it was regular. In 1930 they got an extra 1/- a day. In 1931 we were deep into the Depression, and my seniority at Exeter was further undermined by an influx of young firemen from South Wales sheds who had avoided unemployment by accepting demotion to cleaner; they were redundant at their home depots. This was due to the severe depression of trade, which had greatly reduced demand for South Wales coal and practically closed down the Welsh iron and steel industries. At the end of the summer workings of 1932 the company introduced a policy of making drivers retire at 60 on their pension[1]

---

[1]. Great Western footplate crews had a good pension fund because, in 1865, the men had started their own Engineman's & Firemen's Mutual Assurance Society and the GWR Directors, under the Chairmanship of their ex-Locomotive Superintendent, Daniel Gooch, had supported the men's contributions with annual cash payments. GWR drivers continued to retire at 60 until the outbreak of war in 1939, when they were asked to stay on until they were 65, although they could still retire at 60 if they wished.

and then new drivers were made creating some movement upwards in the grades, so I was able to keep my job as a cleaner.

I worked as a messenger, call boy and office cleaner, on day and night shifts alternately, from July 1929 until the summer workings of 1934. The depression of trade was lifting, and that summer many additional drivers and firemen were required for extra passenger trains: excursions at 1d a mile were run from Exeter to Weston-super-Mare (daytime) and Plymouth or Paignton (evening). Whatever 'Link' a man was in, he was required to move up a grade to cover the extra work of the summer excursions. Senior cleaners — many of them in fact firemen, while others had successfully taken the fireman's exam and were thus 'passed' for firing — were put out firing on yard jobs and trip goods trains so that the existing junior firemen could go out on longer-distance work.

Thus when the 1934 summer workings started I was put into the shed-cleaning gang. A chap called Napper was chargeman cleaner. He was a good all-round chap, knew what was a day's work and wanted it done proper. He was also a family man and had two sons at Exeter shed — one a cleaner, the other a C&W Examiner. This was out in the rough to me, working with 1920/24/26 cleaners, grown men to my 19 years. There were 24 men in each of two gangs, working two turns: 6am to 3pm Monday to Friday, and 6 to 12 and 1.30pm to 10pm on Saturday. We used to get a weekly visit after breakfast from the Railway Chaplain for prayers and hymns.

I had by now saved some cash and put a deposit on a BSA 2¾hp motorcycle to buy it on the never-never. I had this to go to work on early turn and used the train for lates. It also came in handy when I started to get firing turns. This was very different from being in the Offices. I well remember how I as a young hand had to behave with some of these adult cleaners. I suppose they were feeling bad about their lack of promotion but it was best for me never to have anything to say when I was with them in the cabin. When I was having my food they insisted on proper table manners, but they were marvellous chaps for playing tricks on the young ones, throwing oilers at me, pinching my allocation of waste, telling me to go to the foreman's office 'for the long stand' or 'to get the key to the smokebox door'.

I had to cling on the sides of engines' tenders and climb on the tops of boilers, scour the brass and copper with bath brick and

make the green paint look the colour of green leeks. It was real hard work, and I got very oily and dirty cleaning the driving wheels and motions. It had to be done 'proper', though, and the side and coupling rods shone like silver.

I remember the numbers of some of the engines I cleaned: 2905, 2934, 2978, 4006, 4008, 4012, 4018, 4020, 4026, 4040, 4049, 4054, 4061, 4063, 4706, 5003, 5013, 5015, 5026, 5030, 5050 and 5059. These engines were on the London runs, and Exeter men covered London both ways on 'double home', but as more 'Castles' and 'Kings' came out they went to Laira, and that shed got much more of the London work than Exeter did. These bigger engines could take heavier loads through from London to Plymouth and could also cover a greater mileage with one 'prepping'. I can honestly say that when these engines were outside the shed or in the yard after being cleaned they looked great — even our Superintendent passed remarks about them as well as the men working to London and Penzance, Pontypool and Swindon. I watched drivers and firemen do a week's work on these engines, and their overalls were no dirtier on a Saturday than on a Monday.

I was always jumping off heights. Once I jumped off the boiler of a 'Star' (or 'Small 40', as we called them). I pitched onto the concrete flooring of the shed and damaged my instep arches — I had to have treatment because I went flat-footed as a duck. The foot specialist gave me a hell of a time, what with a massage every morning and evening and having to stand in a bucket of cold water afterwards. This went on for six months, after which I could have jumped over the moon.

One of the jobs for Exeter cleaners was to go up the station and bring coal forward in the tenders to help the firemen of certain long-distance trains such as the 'Cornish Riviera', the 'Torbay Express', the up 'Dutchman', up and down Wolverhamptons (later

No 6023 *King Edward II*, barely a year old, rolls majestically into the terminus at Kingswear in the summer of the dreadful year of 1931. In spite of the recession the GWR found the money to build bigger and better engines.
Adrian Vaughan collection

Newton Abbot lads clean No 4099 *Kilgerran Castle* in the 1950s. Note the shiny/dirty state of the safety-valve cover. Sadly, research with old hands has failed to identify any of the young men involved.
John Ashman FRPS

Newton Abbot shed yard on 18 May 1958. Locomotives from left to right are Nos 1023 *County of Oxford*, 4089 *Donnington Castle* (with 5195 behind and 7000 *Viscount Portal* behind that), 5108, 6988 *Swithland Hall*, 5154 and 4145.
courtesy Hugh Ballantyne

No 6023 backs off its train and into the locomotive yard at Kingswear.
Adrian Vaughan collection

the 'Cornishman') and the 1.30 and 3.30 Paddingtons, because these were non-stop Paddington–Exeter or Bristol–Exeter. Through this I got to know a number of engine crews from Old Oak, Bristol and Laira. On a Sunday we cleaners had to pump water from 5am till 7am for the engines going out that morning. We also worked on the coal stage, and did fire cleaning and fire dropping. I would clean a fire on a 'Castle' which came on shed each evening, and then the shed turner would place it for coal and we'd coal it with him helping us. The turner would then put it into the shed yard for the Exeter crew to prepare, and they'd then work it on the up Postal (6.45pm Paddington–Penzance).

As a cleaner I didn't do very well for firing turns during the summers of 1934/5 because of the number of 1920, 1924 and 1926 cleaners from South Wales and Exeter who were senior to me. This was shrewd housekeeping by the company. The senior cleaners from South Wales and the senior Exeter cleaners were on 8/- a day, and the jobs they were covering would have been 9/6d-a-day jobs. I had 22 firing turns as a cleaner before I was promoted to fireman, on 2 February 1936. My pay check number, which I was to carry until the GWR ceased to be, was 23049.

No 4054 *Princess Charlotte*, with Newton Abbot footplatemen, waits in perfect silence for the 'Right Away' from Kingswear with a Manchester train in the summer of 1931.
Adrian Vaughan collection

Princess Charlotte leads her dignified train away from Kingswear.
Adrian Vaughan collection

2. Fireman at Princetown

I was posted to Princetown as a fireman on 2 February 1936. How I had looked forward to this day! I booked on at Exeter at 8am and travelled to Plymouth, where I caught the 12.15pm train to Launceston, getting off at Yelverton for the 2.50pm for Princetown and arriving there at 3.30pm. The branch was about 10½ miles long. The scenery at Burrator Reservoir was out of this world, and, circling around Ingra Tor and King Tor, it was a long pull up to Princetown around all the curves. At Swell Tor I looked out of the coach window and looked down onto the line, far below where we'd come from; it looked like a Hornby train set. At Princetown the stationmaster met me and introduced me to the late-turn train crew: the guard, Frank Price, and the young-hand driver, Gough, with his fireman, Ball, whose place I was taking. I was immediately offered lodgings by Driver Gough, which I gladly accepted. He took me across to his house which was just outside the station — the garden backed onto the line — and introduced me to his wife. She

showed me my bedroom and gave me a cup of tea. Having drunk that I put on my overalls and went to ride on the train engine with Gough and Ball up to Yelverton and back to Princetown to see how the job was done. The branch engines had water lubrication on the flanges of the leading and trailing driving wheel because of the very sharp curves on the line — 180° around King Tor — and the top speed anywhere on the line was 20mph.

Apart from learning the road and the firing technique for the branch, I had to perform shed labourers' duties when on late turn: clearing ashpan and smokebox, dropping the fire — none of which was the normal duty for a GWR fireman — cleaning tubes, blowing down the boiler and shovelling ash and clinker from the engine-shed pit, wheelbarrowing it to the dump outside and throwing it up into the ash wagon. I got a little more pay because of this, and such was the case on all these little branch lines. When there was a small maintenance job, like a steam

A 'full house' at Yelverton on 20 December 1955. The view, in pouring Dartmoor rain, is towards Plymouth. The 12.8pm Princetown branch train has just arrived behind No 4568 to connect — all trains being under one control — with the 12.50pm Tavistock–Plymouth and the 12.49 Plymouth–Launceston hauled by 5567. The Tavistock–Plymouth is formed with No 1408 propelling an 'auto coach'. *courtesy Hugh Ballantyne*

No 4402, the Princetown branch engine, at Yelverton *c*1934. The branch was steeply graded, with many extremely sharp curves which caused severe heating and wear to the flanges of the driving wheels. In 1931 No 4402 was fitted with a Westinghouse steam-operated air compressor and a can of very light oil. The oil was blown onto the driving wheel flanges to ease their passage around 180° curves. Not surprisingly the same oil also reduced the driving wheels' grip on the rail, causing wheelslip, and the equipment had been removed in favour of gravity-fed water by the time Bob Nicks arrived. In 1939 No 4402 encountered a fallen tree and suffered the loss of its chimney. *Stephenson Locomotive Society*

Driver Gough, 20 years older than when Bob fired to him, at Princetown on 2 July 1955. In his left hand he has the electric train staff for the section to Dousland and his can of tea. Next to him is the stationmaster, who will travel on the train as guard. *R. C. Riley*

joint to be packed, or a gland, the engine went into the shed and the senior driver, Driver Mounts saw to it.

Fireman Ball remained to coach me till Thursday and then left for his new shed . . .

Princetown was, as you can imagine, the most bleak and stormswept place for a railway station; it seemed to be on top of the world [2], and February was about the worst time to be introduced to it. Cold winds blew and for long parts of the day from October to April it could be dark as a bag up there in the clouds. Of course, there were bright spring days and hot days in summer, but my strongest impression is of wind and rain and dark. Because the gales were so fierce, Princetown shed was issued with flare lamps with a 2in wick — twice the usual size — and even then the wind could just blow them out like candles. At the end of the day the engine was run to the shed. Whilst it was still outside, the boiler was filled with the injectors, the smokebox was shovelled out and the fire was cleaned of ash and clinker; the remaining fire was left under the brick arch at the front of the grate to keep the

---

[2]. Princetown station was the highest in England, at 1,360ft. Dent was then the second-highest, at 1,145ft.

engine warm and make the basis for quick lighting-up in the morning. Also, during the winter, the frost on the moor was terrible, so it was good policy to keep a very small amount of fire in the grate. The engine was then run into the shed, with the ashpans full, dampers closed, regulator closed, engine in mid-gear, steam cocks open and handbrake on.

Next morning the early turn fireman booked on at 4am, and that was grim in February and March. He cleared the cold ashes from the ashpan into the pit and added some fresh coal to what was left of the fire. While that burned through he cleaned the engine and went back to put some more coal on the fire, building it up, not 'blacking it out'. At 6.30 the driver would arrive to oil round. By 7am you'd be ready to move off shed to get coal. The wooden coaling shack was at the other end of the siding from the engine shed. It was open to north winds but protected from warm, south winds. The engine was coaled by hand from a wagon alongside the platform. Coaling the bunker when the wind was whistling across the moor was murder. You could put gallons of water on it, but the black dust still blew into your eyes and nose.

Two evenings a week we were rostered to pump water into the supply tank which supplied the station toilets and the railway houses for toilets and washing. The water was crystal-clear, icy

cold and good for drinking. I had no trouble with the boiler of 4402, no priming, and it was well known that Princetown branch engines could go for weeks longer between washouts than the official time. What did get them into Laira in the end was the wheel flanges, which had to be checked for wear.

I soon made some good friends at Princetown and stopped feeling homesick for my mother's cooking. There were always social functions going on in the village — concerts, whist drives etc — and there were four pubs selling a grade of beer that was 4d a pint. There was also the bar at the railway staff club, and railway staff were always welcomed at the prison officers' club, which I joined.

If you were working early turn and wanted to get into Plymouth you could not leave till 4pm. You got to Plymouth at 5.15pm and the train back to Princetown left at 6.15, arriving Princetown at 7.35. There was no public transport but the train, so I took my motorcycle out there. There was no Sunday service, and on Saturdays one fireman would work from 4am to 10.30pm so as to give his mate the whole weekend off. On my motorcycle I visited Moretonhampstead and Tavistock, but I was wary of being out on the moor because of fog and snow and the dark in the winter. You could leave Princetown in lashing rain and thick mist and go down the hill a mile or two and run into bright, spring sun.

I had been at Princetown six or seven weeks. It was an early Easter, and on the Good Friday we were off duty. The sky began to darken with a huge black cloud coming in from the west; it got blacker and lower and darker, and around 9am snow started falling. By noon it was a foot deep on the ground. We could not work on the Saturday, and on the Sunday the snowplough was worked over the branch to clear it for Bank Holiday Monday.

A new halt, Ingra Tor, was opened for the visitors on 2 March 1936. There were slate quarries nearby and a few isolated houses for the quarrymen, and many walks around. It was beautiful when the weather was right, and as spring advanced I really enjoyed the work, going up and down the branch, seeing the lake sparkling below, and climbing up to Princetown as if it was on top of the world.

Come the end of May I was called back to Newton Abbot, and I left Princetown glad to be going back to what I hoped would be main-line work, yet sad to be leaving behind a beautiful place and some very good friends.

What is going on here? The 11.19am Yelverton–Princetown stops at Ingra Tor halt on 20 December 1955. The rain is streaming down and the guard is not inclined to stick his head out too far but gives an automatic green flag to the fireman. But Hugh Ballantyne has thoughtfully left his door open and the fireman and driver, looking back for the guard, can see this and do not move, whilst smiling broadly at the guard's mystification. *Hugh Ballantyne*

After 10½ miles' tortuous climbing, the 11.19am Yelverton has finally arrived at Princetown, the highest railway station in England.
Hugh Ballantyne

3. Junior Fireman at Newton Abbot

No 5067 *St.Fagans Castle* passing Clink Road Junction on the 'cut-off' line with the third part of the 3.30pm Paddington–Penzance in August 1936. In the holiday season it was normal for the regular express to have up to four 'parts' so as to prevent the passengers being uncomfortably overcrowded. *John Hayward / Adrian Vaughan collection*

No 6012 *King Edward VI* comes out of Westbury and approaches Fairwood Junction with a down West of England express in 1936. The Westbury avoiding line, opened in 1933, is on the right. *John Hayward / Adrian Vaughan collection*

I returned to Newton Abbot for the summer workings 1936 due to a number of extra trains which made it very busy in the holidays. Being a junior I was put in the Yard 'Cripple' Link to cover shunting duties with drivers who had failed eyesight or were medically undergrade. I had a good old mate called Tom Rowe who was a real socialist. He used to look after the Labour Club gardens and recruited me to the Labour Party, in which I have remained ever since. He also used to like a bet on the horses and followed the trainer Jack Jarvis. I had some happy times with him. During this summer a number of 1916 and 1917 firemen were promoted to drivers and were posted to South Wales. I was lucky and remained at Newton Abbot, and was promoted into the Junior Yard Link. This link had 24 turns. We covered the trips between goods yards, as well as carriage shunting and shed turning, but we also worked trains to Plymouth, Kingswear and Exeter, and I began to collect a very good knowledge of the roads (railway routes) locally. I had some good mates who were very interested in the engines and who were regular class attenders before they passed as drivers, so they were on top of their work and a number of them

were Improvement Class instructors. This class was held during the winter timetable every Sunday morning in the shed and there would be 60 and sometimes even 70 people attending.

Some of my drivers in the Junior Yard Link were W. Bowden, W. Warren, J. Blair and E. Tranter, all of whom were fine. However, there was one other driver whom I never got on with. He never stopped finding fault with my work — everything had to be just right for him. The engine cab had to be kept clean and polished, the coal must never be dusty but I must never use much water to damp it. Yet he had no idea of how to drive a steam engine, and on some days he would be three parts cut with beer and cider, especially on Newton Abbot market day. It is true that 'when the beer is in the wit is out', and he became dangerous when he was in this mood and state. He would do spiteful things: if we were running backwards on a bunker engine, he would close the regulator when I was firing. I only got caught once: we were on 4587 and he shut down; the fire fumes billowed out, burning the hairs off my hands and my eyebrows and singeing my hair. The smell of burnt hair was all about me, so he couldn't deny it had happened.

When we got back to Newton I went directly to the foreman, Mr Sheppard, and reported the incident. If I had gone to the Superintendent, this driver would have lost his job, and I had some thought for his wife and children, who led a hell of a life with him as it was. Mr Sheppard gave him a good dressing-down and sent him home for a week without pay, and the higher people never heard about it. But the family went on short rations.

Shortly after this I moved on, due to a tragic event on our shed in which a driver, oiling under the boiler, was squashed by the big-ends. The handbrake had not been applied on the engine next to the one that was being oiled (which did have its brake on). An engine was being moved by the shed turner, a passed fireman. He buffered against the unbraked engine which

No 6029 *King Edward VIII* arriving at Bristol with a two-coach stopping train from Swindon via Badminton in 1937. This was a running-in turn for the engine, which had just emerged from overhaul in Swindon Works.
John Hayward / Adrian Vaughan collection

rolled off and hit the one with the driver under the boiler. Because of this a Senior Shed Link was formed, and I joined it. We had 12 turns, with train work to Exeter, Kingswear and Plymouth when not working on the shed as turners. In this link I had two mates to fire to, Warren and Webb. It was marvellous to be working with these men; they were good-humoured, skilful drivers who had consideration for the fireman and the engine.

The next link for me was the 'Senior Cripple' or Banking Link, with six turns. The drivers in this link had been in No 1 Link but, having about 18 months to go before retirement, could apply for this light work. We did local passenger work to Exeter and Kingswear and a goods turn to Brixham. It was a very good link — interesting work, no early starts, and finishing at 9.30pm latest. My regular mate was Fred ('Fuzzy') Furze. From here I moved into the Bank Engine Link, with Ern Chandler. He came from an all-railway family: his father was a driver and his brother a fireman at Taunton. I had already worked with Ern for a short while in the Junior Yard Link, so we were no strangers. Ern liked a pint or two of beer or cider, but he was sensible about it, and good-natured. Our work consisted of banking duties at Aller Junction and Totnes and piloting to/from Plymouth, both passenger and freight. We also

One of the powerful '47xx' class at rest inside Old Oak Common shed in 1960. The scene remained largely unchanged for 40 years and was one very familiar to Bob Nicks. *Adrian Vaughan collection*

The scene at the west end of Bristol Temple Meads station during the changeover from mechanical to power-operated signalling in 1934. A 'Hall' waits alongside a 'Saint', both with West of England expresses. *John Hayward / Adrian Vaughan collection*

worked freight over the Ashburton branch, coal and mineral trains to Plymouth, trip work to Hackney Yard and local goods, shunting all stations.

When we were working these all-stations goods or going up the Ashburton branch (10.30am NA, 11.35 ex Totnes) we had the turn for the week, and we often had some happy-go-lucky goods guard — the same man all week as a rule — who used to take a drop of cider. As a rule our man was 'Rocky' Sanders, and he would have a gallon jar in his van. When we got to Buckfastleigh, at about 11.45 (booked 12.10–1.35), he would go to 'The Sailor' to get it filled and bring it back to the engine. We'd share it between the three of us to wash down our bread and cheese, emptying it before we left, and then go on to Ashburton (scheduled arrival 1.45), shunt the yard, and then it was dinner time. We'd go into the 'Exeter Arms' for a couple of jugs of cider to wash down a pasty, then fill the gallon jar again to set us up for the homeward journey (2.35 Ashburton, 5.20/5.45 Totnes, 6.20 arrive NA), making sure the jar was empty before we got to Totnes. This is how we carried on — there were no fall-outs, and we were happy as sandboys. Our engines on this job were 734 and 1650. Reg Webber was the guard we used to have on the Exeter goods, 4.25am from Hackney (7.33am Exeter).

'Bulldog' class No 3383 pilots a 'King' on Dainton Bank onto a length of freshly laid track just above Stoneycombe. The 'King' is passing the speed-restriction warning board. As the picture was taken *c*1938, the 'Bulldog's' fireman could be Bob Nicks.
John Ashman FRPS

He liked a drop of cider any time and we'd call in the 'Railway Arms' at Starcross, where of course I knew the publican, Harry Lovelock. At about 7am I'd go to the back door of the pub and ask him how it was looking for some cider, and he'd sell me a couple of bottles. I'd tell him we'd be on this turn all week. 'Come in every morning,' he'd say. So we'd have our cider with breakfast at Exminster, and on the return journey (9am Exeter) I'd get our flagons filled again at Starcross at
10 o'clock. This would keep us all going till we got back to Hackney about half past one. Reg was one of the best; we had laughs galore and got the job done just the same, and we covered each other so management had no chance to catch anyone out. He and the others of his age were sadly missed when they retired.

The firemen in Bank Engine Link covered the branch firemen's holidays, which meant lodging at Kingsbridge or Moretonhampstead, but at Ashburton there was a late bus after the last train into the terminus and I could get back home. I often covered these branches and had some happy times and made some good friends.

While I was in the Banking Link I was called on to work my first (official) trip to Paddington. It was a very dark and dreary day in November 1939. I was sent for by the foreman, H. Cooke, to

The final preparation after 'oiling round' — setting the fire right, checking everything for roadworthiness. The driver of No 5020 *Trematon Castle* — who bears a striking resemblance to the GWR's ace driver, Jim Street — controls the tap and his fireman watches the rising water level in the tender. The young Bob Nicks was to be up there on the tender by 1940. This scene was captured at Old Oak Common on 29 June 1934 by the GWR's staff photographer.
Adrian Vaughan collection

'Star' No 4060 *Princess Eugenie* with the 9.45 Swansea–Goodrington at Bristol Temple Meads in 1937.
John Hayward/ Adrian Vaughan collection

book on at 12.45pm, prepare an engine and work the 1.20pm Plymouth to Liverpool from Newton to Bristol and then change to the 5.45pm Bristol to Paddington — 'double home'. This was a No 1 Passenger Link job and I was in the Banking Link and had never been beyond Taunton. The engine was 4061 *Glastonbury Abbey*. I was working on the engine when the driver, C. Davis, arrived, and he wondered what I was doing. I told him his mate had been sent home because his wife had been taken ill and that I had been told to take over and would do my best for him. He said: 'I expect you'll do as well as my mate if you do as you're told.' I made sure I did my 'prep' thoroughly — perfectly clean ashpan and smokebox, quite clear of cinders, plenty of dry sand, coal well trimmed, a pair of good flare lamps and a good, clean gauge lamp. As we came off the shed I told him that I did not know the road above Taunton, but he told me not to worry provided I was willing to be told how to carry on. It was experience that counted in footplate work. He was like a father to me on that trip, and many times afterwards I changed with his fireman and went with him.

We coupled onto 12 coaches at the station for 380 tons and

---

[3]. Scrutiny of the GWR's 1936 service timetable reveals they were actually only 20 tons over the limit.

stopped at Teignmouth, Dawlish and Exeter, where we got another three coaches put on — 15 coaches for 470 tons, which was 50 over our limit[3]. My driver was asked if he wanted assistance, but he said 'No' and we trotted off to Taunton, perhaps losing a bit of time, but the engine was great for steam. At Taunton they put another six vans on us, making the load 520 tons, 70 tons over the limit for this class of engine. The Taunton Station Inspector asked if we wanted an assistant engine, but my driver said we'd be all right but we'd drop a bit of time with the stops at Bridgwater, Highbridge and Weston. While we were standing at Taunton we put the anti-glare sheets down and it was dark as a bag inside the cab as well as out — a real November day, although there was no fog.

Driver Davis was very light on the engine, not one of the 'hard hitters'. I fired the engine straight down the middle, well up in the back corners and under the doors so there was a place for my shovel to rest when I was firing to the front corners and under the brick arch. My driver told me to watch the chimney after each firing and if the exhaust went grey after 15 seconds then I had a good hot fire and she'd steam. I worked the exhaust injector when running and kept the water in sight at the top of the glass so the driver could see how much we were using. We arrived in Temple Meads doing well, having covered 96 miles from Newton Abbot.

◀ A 'B'-headcode passenger train, which appears also to be a parcels train, stopping all stations Plymouth–Newton Abbot. No 6861 *Crynant Grange* pilots a 'Hall' up the 1-in-170 gradient off Blatchford Viaduct, east of Cornwood station. *Peter Barlow / Adrian Vaughan collection*

I remember thinking: 'If I can keep things up like this I shan't have a lot of trouble getting to Paddington!'

We handed over 4061 and went to the next engine. We left Bristol for Paddington via Bath with 15 for 470 tons. Driver Davis was offered a pilot engine to Swindon but refused it, and I thought what confidence he had, with Box Tunnel and Wootton Bassett Incline ahead. I was going to places I had never seen, had no knowledge of the road or the signals and had to cope with the added awkwardness of working underneath the anti-glare screens. We stopped at Bath, Chippenham, Swindon, Didcot and Reading. As we passed Langley my driver told me to start to let the fire run down — so as not to be blowing off steam standing at Paddington — and we arrived there about 26 minutes late.

I felt pretty tired but I was very pleased with my trip. Driver Davis told me I had done as well as a No 1 Link fireman working the job regularly, because we'd worked on superheated steam all the way, with the water always showing in the glass, and I'd always used the exhaust injector to put boiling water into the boiler. He told me these things as we stood on the buffers, still coupled to our stock waiting to be pulled out to the carriage sidings where we would cut off and go to Old Oak Common. He praised me for my efforts and wished me luck in my future career. He also said:

◀ No 2891 emerges from Dainton Tunnel with a down coal train, with steam shut off and brakes applied, in 1957. Inside the short tunnel the gradient changes from 1 in 44 (rising) to 1 in 36 (falling), and continues downhill for some miles thereafter at steep gradients. All down, unbraked freight trains had to stop outside Dainton signalbox to allow the guard to pin down a sufficient number of handbrakes on the wagons, to control the weight of the train; the engine brake and guard's handbrake were not enough. This is the legacy Brunel left the railway by choosing this route for his ill-fated 'atmospheric' railway. *Peter Barlow / Adrian Vaughan collection*

21

A 'Hall' passes Torquay Gas Sidings with a down train, seen from opposite the signalbox in August 1937. *John Hayward / Adrian Vaughan collection*

Things were practically unchanged 21 years later, and still working well. Gloucester-based No 7926 *Willey Hall* brings the 8.10am Newport–Paignton past Torquay Gas Sidings 'box on 14 June 1958. *courtesy S. C. Nash*

'I hope this isn't a case of a new broom sweeping clean. If you keep up the standards you've shown me today you'll have a good career on the footplate.' He went on: 'When we go home tomorrow you'll have the biggest test of your life — we've got the 1.30 Padd, and that will be a "King".'

When we got back to Old Oak shed we were put on the Yard Stores line to dispose of our engine. I had never seen so many engines or so many fire pit lines filled up, and the size of the place, the booking-on hall and the number of men in the hall or in the cabins... There were four turntable sheds joined as one. It amazed me. We booked off about 10pm and went to our lodgings in Wells House Road, where we had a good wash and a bit of supper before going off to bed.

After a good night's sleep I had a good breakfast and then walked back to Old Oak shed for 11am. This was one hour before our signing-on time; as I did not know my way around the shed, Driver Davis thought it best I have plenty of time for preparation.

In the booking-on hall were all the roster duty sheets, covering 1,500 sets of men. The 'double home' men were on a separate sheet, and we found we had 6003 *King George IV* booked to us. It was a nice morning, overcast but dry and the shed roof had a large area of glass which kept it warm at that time of year — although I later found that it got hellish hot in summer. No 6003 was under the roof, on a spur from the turntable. I quietly set about preparing our engine. I carefully examined the smokebox, the tube ends and the boiler plugs for leaks and cleared the box of 'conkers'. Then I screwed up the door good and tight and swept the ashes off the front footplate. I made sure we had our tools, spanners, bucket, brush, irons and detonators, and that the tender handbrake was screwed down hard. Driver Davis then went underneath to oil up and I prepared my fire, spreading it all over the bars.

When it was our time to move onto the turntable, the shed driver gave my mate the tip to come on so we could turn our tender to face Paddington and then move out of the shed. By then it was good to get out in the fresh air and move to the water column. I had a good fire and 240lb on the clock, and I tried both injectors. I put the bag in and kept the right-hand injector on. I washed down the footplate, being careful to keep the driver's side dry because he didn't want to stand on damp boards. I damped the coal with water from the bag and then gave the coal a good trimming. We had a supply of coal I thought would take us to Plymouth. So now we were ready to leave the shed at about 12.50. My driver told me where to 'ask off' the shed, giving engine number and train working. [Young Bob surely felt good when he reported in: '6003 for the 1.30 Penzance'.] We set off along the up Engine & Carriage line with three other sets of men travelling to Paddington on the engine, and arrived at Platform 3. I coupled the engine onto the train and saw that we were right on the end of the platform, opposite the Departure box. I took the lamp off the tender and collected another lamp from the engine and put up 'A' headlights on the front, one over each buffer. Both lamps were lit. Driver Davis tried the vacuum which was OK. He said to me again: 'You'll be able to test your skill with a "King" — we've got 15 or 16 on and it's 143 miles to the first stop.' The guard then came up and said we had '16 for 528 tons'. That was 28 tons over the permitted load to Newton Abbot, and 43 tons over load for Wellington Bank.

Driver Davis told me to put more coal on and turn up the blower and open the two back dampers. I had a good pot of water and we were on the blow at 250lb when we started. I pulled the long poker around the fire to fill up any holes made by the fire burning and then let the fire burn through with the blower on. The grate got hot, and passing Old Oak Common I turned off the blower and started to fire, keeping the fire well up at the back. I soon found out the difference between 4061 and this engine[4], but 6003 was a London engine; the tubes were clean and it blew its head off. I was able to go along with the fire door flap open and the exhaust injector running. My driver gave me confidence by knocking the engine about a bit. After Southall we were running at about 75mph.

---

[4] Bob is referring to the larger, longer firebox.

We were certainly keeping good time and we got into Taunton on time. Now I was on my home ground and having no trouble with two coaches over the load on Wellington Bank. We got to Newton Abbot on time but I was rather black. I had shovelled some 4 or 5 tons of coal and I was glad of relief. The driver was full of praise for my handling of this first 'double home' trip to London, and a number of drivers were making mention of it.

After this I often changed my turns with Driver Davis's fireman and went with him on 'double home' trips, to Swansea and Shrewsbury. During my time as a fireman in the Junior Link I liked to travel, and a number of firemen would change turns with me rather than doing a 'double home' to Shrewsbury, London or Swansea, if their driver mates were agreeable (they always were). I was a strong chap with plenty of vigour, and I had a wonderful experience, firing all classes of locomotive and gaining valuable route knowledge about the position of signals and the names of all the stations and signalboxes. These name boards were taken down or blacked out during the war, but my mates instructed me and this stood me in good stead when I became a driver.

At times we in the Junior Link were called upon officially to cover No 4 Main Line Link. This involved freight turns to Bristol or Westbury when a senior fireman was taken off his 'double home' freight turn to cover a Paddington or Penzance 'double home' passenger turn. So as a young fireman at Newton Abbot I had good work, and by covering the No 4 Link I found myself firing 'Kings', 'Castles' and 'Stars' on occasion, as well as 'Halls', 'Granges', 'Manors', '31xx', '41xx', '45xx', '55xx' and others. The drivers I had were good men and were willing to teach me how to carry on, ie the Rules and the 'ins and outs' of the different classes.

▲ No 6018 *King Henry VI* strolls away up the bank from Torquay with a stopping train for Kingswear on August Bank Holiday 1937. The engine will probably work back on a heavy express to Paddington.
John Hayward /
Adrian Vaughan collection

Bob also fired Moretonhampstead branch trains. This is Heathfield, four miles from Newton Abbot, looking north to the junction for the Teign Valley line and Moretonhampstead, *c*1953. The Moretonhampstead–Newton Abbot 'push-pull' train is nearest the camera, with the Teign Valley branch train standing behind to make the connection. Normally this train would be a 'push-pull', but today a pannier is standing in with a couple of ordinary coaches.
Adrian Vaughan collection

Moretonhampstead station yard, looking towards Newton Abbot, on 7 February 1959. The engine shed, with signal-box attached, is on the right.
Adrian Vaughan collection

No 1466, now preserved at Didcot Railway Centre, takes water in the yard at Moretonhampstead on 7 February 1959. It is attached to its carriage, 'trailer' or 'auto coach'. The latter was equipped with a driving cab at the outer end. This journey to Newton Abbot will be made with the driver working from the leading end of the 'auto coach'.
Adrian Vaughan collection

Signalman Evans with, over his shoulder, the steel hoop carrying the electric train token, the key to the single line as far as Bovey. No train can enter the single track without its token, and Mr Evans will hand it up to the driver as he passes.
Adrian Vaughan collection

No 5196 waits to depart Moretonhampstead for Newton Abbot on 7 February 1959.
Adrian Vaughan collection

No 1470, shedded at Newton Abbot, standing under the roof of Ashburton station with the 3.35 departure for Totnes on 14 August 1956. Alongside is an 'auto coach' carrying the 'Totnes' destination board. The station building is very similar to that at Moreton-hampstead. Both these branch lines were closely associated with the South Devon Railway, a satellite of the Great Western, and the station architecture has strongly Brunelian influences in its design, although it was erected several years after Brunel's death.
Hugh Ballantyne

Heathfield signalbox and the Teign Valley Line (to the right), seen from a Moretonhampstead-bound train *c*1953.
Adrian Vaughan collection

Buckfastleigh station, 2½ miles south of Ashburton, on 15 February 1958, with No 1427 working the 2.45pm (SO) to Totnes. Most unusually, the passenger accommodation consists of an ex-LMS Brake Third, rather than an ex-GWR 'auto coach'.
Hugh Ballantyne

No 5557 standing at Newton Abbot up platform in the summer of 1937. The footplateman must surely have been a friend of Bob's.
Adrian Vaughan collection

4. Senior Fireman

I became a senior fireman when I moved into No 4 Link in 1941. My mate in this link was 'Brother' Lew Dowton, who was another who liked his cider, and knew where all the pubs were when we were in a loop. He was happy-go-lucky, and was well known at all the depots. When we were in the cabins at one depot or another the chaps used to get him going to sing. One song was 'I am an Airman', which he sang with his gas mask and steel helmet on!

Now we were doing very long hours on freight — real hard (but varied) work. We worked to Bristol, Westbury and Plymouth, and thought nothing of being on duty for 15 hours continuously. During 1940 we'd be on a goods to Westbury or Bristol and we'd look up and see the sky full of Jerry's planes up at a terrific height with our planes amongst them. When they were raiding Bristol there would be trains in every loop from Hackney to Bristol West Depot and you could spend eight hours

Wearing gasmasks and capes to protect their lungs and bodies from mustard-gas attack, locomen of Newton Abbot shed attend to a bomb casualty. This was First Aiding in 1940. Robert Nicks is the 'victim'. *courtesy Ivy Nicks*

▲ getting from one end of Huish Loop to the other. At times I'd be on duty for 30 hours and I'd eat next day's food and have nothing left to come home with. It used to get me down, but my driver, F. Williams, knew what war was — he'd had a rough time in the 1914-18 war, so he was hardened to it. And of course we got the overtime, and we'd be booked on the Moretonhampstead or Kingswear line trains the next turn as a rest cure.

When my turns took me to Bristol, we would book off at St Philip's Marsh shed and from there I'd walk to my lodge with my brother-in-law, Ron Cumes, in St Anne's Park. He was GWR salaried staff in the Divisional Offices in Bristol, but we didn't have many disagreements! I had some lucky escapes in the early hours, during air raids, on the way to or from St Philip's Marsh. I was in Bristol during some heavy raids — I even spent nights in

the dug-out in the garden rather than in bed asleep. There was some devastating bombing. I saw the city lit up like daylight with the fires and the searchlights and the flashes from the anti-aircraft guns in action, with the shrapnel falling in great chunks and doing its own damage.

During 1941, promotion at Newton Abbot was rapid, due to the number of drivers required. I went into the Senior Freight Link firing 'C'- and 'D'-headcode trains to Bristol, Westbury and Penzance, still on 'double home'. Many men did not like 'double homing', and management and unions were even then in discussions about how to abolish it — at least on freight workings. Most of our 'double home' freight working was done away with in 1941, and most of Newton Abbot's freight work was then restricted to Taunton one way and Tavistock Junction–Plymouth the other. We did, however, retain a couple of 'C'-headcode trains to Bristol and Westbury to maintain the route knowledge, but we no longer worked beyond Plymouth — that work went to Laira and Penzance. This new system was good, because, as the war went on, it took 12 or 15 hours to get to Taunton, so it was as well we were not required to work further east.

I had about 12 months in the Senior Freight Link, and then in 1942 I went into No 2 Link, which was all passenger work to London (both ways), Penzance, Shrewsbury and Swansea, and spare turns. We also covered for No 1 Link vacancies. This was great, because there was extra cash for mileage beyond the standard day of 140 miles. I spent 2½ years in this link, having a good all-round, happy-go-lucky mate, Frank Bowden. He was a wonderful character. He liked his pint of beer and carried a quart of cider when we went to London on a day job. He was a bit of a 'hard hitter' but it was all the same to Frank — good trips or bad trips when the engine wouldn't steam because the boiler was dirty. He would say to me: 'You keep the needle of your clock pointing my way, Bob, and we'll keep moving.' This man had no fear with plenty or with little water in the boiler, but as a fireman I never had any plugs go. Frank would never give an engine up if it was steaming rough unless it was completely hopeless — 'It's better to keep the devil you know,' he used to say.

I never knew Frank in a bad temper — he was always pleasant and jolly, and wonderful company. Off duty in London we travelled miles together on the Underground. We went to loads of theatres, trying them all — the Victoria Palace and the Palladium, the Haymarket, Shepherd's Bush Empire, Chiswick Empire, Golders Green Empire — and when we'd had enough of those comedians we often used to go to the House of Commons Public Gallery to hear a debate. During the spring and summer we would have a boat trip on the Thames or go to Kew Gardens We'd go to mid-week soccer matches, and if we did a Friday midnight turn out of Newton and booked off at Old Oak on a Saturday morning we'd have some sleep and then go to watch Arsenal or Chelsea or West Ham in the afternoon. On Sundays we went down Petticoat Lane for the street market or to Hyde Park Corner to hear the soap-box wallahs. We went to cricket at The Oval, racing at Kempton and greyhound racing at Wembley. On our way back to our lodgings at 44 Wells House Road we'd call in for a pint and a game of darts at the 'Fisherman's Arms' near Old Oak shed or 'The Castle' in North Acton. Frank was a brilliant darts player.

No 44 Wells House Road, off Old Oak Common Road, Robert's regular lodge on the 'double home' turns, photographed 55 years after the bombs, land mines and V2 rockets stopped falling. *Adrian Vaughan*

For the more fastidious Great Western or Western Region footplateman — a steam-heated immersion heater for boiling water for tea. The device consists of a spiral of copper tube with an internally threaded butterfly nut. The latter was screwed onto the steam lance connection on the smoke box. The spiral was immersed in the water-filled tea can and boiler steam was admitted through the steam-lance tap. In the picture, steam through the heater can be seen escaping across the front of the engine. This device was the alternative to the more usual — and cruder — method of tea-making: putting the water-filled tea can on the shovel and into the firebox. This violent heat 'stewed' the tea horribly and made the exterior of the can filthy black, extremely hot and difficult to handle. The portable immersion heater was made up — for a consideration — by the shed boilersmith and was unique to the Great Western/ Western Region because no other railway provided its engines with properly tapped access to boiler steam. The smokebox connection was, officially, for the steam lance. Coupled to the connector by a length of flexible hose, the lance could be used to direct a high-velocity jet of steam through the boiler tubes to clear them of soot and cinders, or could be used to blow ice and snow out of points. The steam-era GWR/WR was a sublimely well organised concern. *courtesy Newton Abbot Town & GWR Museum*

After the Luftwaffe's 'Baedekker' raid on Bath, No 6001 King Edward VII tests the rapid repair to a huge crater in the track alongside Lower Bristol Road on 15 May 1942. The Divisional Officers arrived not by motor car but riding in their dignified saloon. *Adrian Vaughan collection*

▲ Whilst in No 2 Link I did any amount of London work, even other men's turns. I think the only thing I did not like about these lodging turns was getting into a bed still warm from the man who had just got out of it. There was a shortage of lodging accommodation, and many men would have to use what accommodation there was. But No 44 had a kind landlady, Hilda, and there were times when I cleaned her windows for her and she paid me with a bottle of beer. Because the war was on and there were air raids, many of our men did not like going, but I thought it was a good gain if you could do seven hours' work and get paid for 13 because of the mileage enhancement, and I could put up with the hot bed. Frank Bowden was well in with the foreman at Newton Abbot, Mr Sheppard; they had been buddies since they were cleaners at Port Talbot, and they were both blinking good railwaymen. There was plenty of extra work at Newton, and, if a spare mileage turn cropped up when Frank and I were on some local turn, Mr Sheppard would take us off that and put us on the mileage job for Paddington or Swansea. The extra shillings were very welcome as I had got married by then and had a little daughter and a baby son.

During my time in No 2 Link I worked hard to brush up on the Rules and the workings of the engines so as to pass for a driver.

My wife, Ivy, used to help me with this. We'd sit down in the kitchen and she have the Rule Book, and by looking at a Rule she could turn it round into a question. She did the same with the books on engine failures.

While in this link I worked as a fireman on a Royal Train a couple of times. Both times I fired to Driver Davis and both times we had 5034 *Corfe Castle*, once with King George VI from Totnes onto the Ashburton branch for the night and once from Totnes to Plymouth Millbay. Of all the 'Castles' and 'Kings' at Newton Abbot, 5034 was my favourite engine.

Another trip I had with Driver Davis was working the 4.49pm Newton Abbot–Bristol (12.15pm Penzance–Crewe passenger and mail) with 6007. We would unhook our engine at Bristol and stand by to work the 7.35 Bristol–Paddington (via Bath). On this particular evening we got to Flax Bourton and were given Air Raid 'Red' for Bristol — ie we were to proceed at reduced speed and obey all signals. We got to Temple Meads at about 7.30, stood off the train and waited on a through line for the Weston. The sirens were wailing, anti-aircraft guns were firing, and there was not a soul at Temple Meads but me and my driver — all the passengers and staff had gone to air-raid shelters. We were sitting in the cab of 6007 when there was a hell of a bang. Our 'King' actually rocked in the force of the blast wave. Jerry had dropped one in the LMS station[5]. It caused great damage over that side, blowing out signals and telephones. The raid ended about 10.20pm and we left Bristol at about 10.40, travelling at reduced speed and being prepared to stop short of any obstruction.

At Foxes Wood 'box we had the distant and home on. I went to the 'box and the signalman was in a state of fright. He had no light — only his hand lamp and a small fire burning. I knocked on the door and at first he would not let me in, but I banged harder and he unlocked it. He had been in his iron shelter since just after 7pm. He told me he had heard bangs and bumps all around and now had no bells or telephones working either to Bristol or Keynsham. 'Perhaps a bomb has fallen on the line between here and Keynsham,' I suggested. He asked me what to do (!) and I said I would report back to my driver. Driver Davis said it would be best to proceed with me walking in front of the engine and

---

[5] Bob is using the slang term for Platforms 13, 14 and 15, used mainly by LMS local trains to Gloucester or Bath (Green Park).

calling him on. We told the signalman what we would do and explained the position to the guard.

From Foxes Wood to Keynsham the line is straight after you get out of the woods and the cutting, and once into the open you can see Keynsham and the chocolate factory. I could see the fields in the dark. There were a couple of large craters in one field, one of which was close to the railway; it was here that the wires had been blown down and the posts uprooted, but the track was OK so I waved my mate on to where I was standing. The train came on, and eventually we got to Keynsham. The signalman here was in his iron shelter. He had had no relief and was very upset by events. He had no communications either, so we carried on to Saltford and from there to Bath. Being some four to five hours late at this stage, we could not make up time, and I think we finally booked off at Old Oak Common around 8am, about 10 hours late. We worked home with the 6.30pm Paddington–Penzance via Bath, instead of the 4.15pm.

Another trip I recall was with Driver MacNamara and 6026 with 525 tons on the 9.50pm 'Padd-Penz'. It was a July night with a full moon, and there was a lot of enemy air activity. We went slowly enough but had no trouble, getting to Bristol safe but late and leaving at around 3am. As we were passing Uphill Junction we saw flaming trails of rockets going up from the South Wales coast. We kept going steady with our eyes and ears open. Dawn was breaking as we passed Highbridge. We had a 5mph caution over the river bridge near Huntspill, and passed over it at walking speed. I was looking forward through my window and — lo and behold! — just above the front of the engine was a fighter-bomber with the swastika on its tail coming straight at us. He banked and turned and opened his guns, punching holes in the top and side of the tender and knocking out windows in the parcels vans nearest the engine. We didn't stop and we just hoped this client wouldn't either. Looking across the Bristol Channel to South Wales we could see they were having a battle — the whole sky seemed to be filled with planes, ours and the enemy's.

We carried on to Bridgwater, where we were stopped by a signalman who told us there was an air raid on! We told him we knew what was on, and got down to examine the engine for damage. The tender was holed and water was flowing out merrily, but otherwise there was little damage, and we decided to continue; we were able to take water at Creech troughs. At Taunton we left

the two leading vehicles in the yard and took more water at the column. We carried on with the same engine, took yet more water at Exeter and at Exminster troughs and got safely to Newton, where we took the engine to the shed.

Today we hear a lot about the speed of the diesels, but the 'Kings' and the 'Castles' could go, and Frank Bowden was a speed ace. Of course, during the war years speed was very restricted, but time was often made up to get home. I well remember a weekend in June when Frank Bowden and I had worked up from Newton on a Saturday with the 'Torbay' and back next day with the 10.30 'Limited'. Frank looked at the roster sheets at Old Oak and found we had 6014. 'This is the streamline one,' he said, 'the one with bullet nose[6]. We'll try him down from Savernake through Lavington.' I was all for it. When we got to Paddington we found we had 15 coaches waiting for us and were not due to stop until Exeter. We were lucky with the road that night and it was no trouble at all to reach 80 before Reading. After Savernake my mate let it go and — without telling any tales — going through Lavington the speedo was showing 97 and remained there till we had to brake for Heywood Road Junction. After Castle Cary he opened it out again and we were over 90 down through Somerton to Athelney. We had no p-way checks and we were 21 minutes

---

[6] The streamlining was removed from this locomotive in January 1943.

Streamlined No 6014 *King Henry VII* runs into Paignton past the North signalbox on August Bank Holiday 1937. *John Hayward/ Adrian Vaughan collection*

A Plymouth–Manchester express at Hereford. Porters have unloaded a young tree (amongst other things) from the van, two men are standing at the compartment window, lighting their cigarettes, and a large farewell party has congregated at the end compartment. The left-hand figure of the group appears to be overcome with emotion.
courtesy Russell Mulford

Paddington, 25 July 1943. The 'Torbay Express' — shabby but unbeaten — waits to leave with a load of holidaymakers and a soldier being seen off by his family.
Adrian Vaughan collection

early into Exeter. Of course, the official limit for all trains during the war was 60mph. These engines were masters of any job, so long as they were properly serviced and had the right coal.

The worst conditions for footplatemen were fog, snow and extreme cold. The anti-air-raid blackout created an additional hazard because you could not show a light if you were attending to anything in the open, or going to use a lineside telephone.

If you were doing rough for steam the anti-glare screen was a great nuisance when you were trying to use the long bar with 'Kings' and 'Castles'.

During the war intermediate electric signals were placed inside the Severn Tunnel [7]. The distant signal was about ¾ mile inside, and the stop signal much further on. This consisted of two red lights, one above the other. There was an ATC ramp which gave you a siren when it was at 'Danger', which was very helpful, but we still had great difficulty in finding it, with the smoke as thick as a bag from the trains. If you were stopped you'd have to get down and go to the 'phone. The tunnel was freezing cold, pitch-dark and full of thick smoke; it wasn't much of a place to be groping about for a telephone, and if your engine was blowing off steam you could hardly hear yourself speak, let alone what the signalman told you to do. The best way to enter the tunnel was with the clock off the mark and the injector on.

Out in the open, fog was very hazardous, and sometimes you couldn't see the front of

[7]. This was done in November 1941 to halve the length of the block section formed by the tunnel and thus permit a greater number of trains to pass through in the same period of time.

A Manchester–Plymouth waiting to depart from Hereford in 1957, with No 5073 *Blenheim* and Newton Abbot men in charge. *courtesy Russell Mulford*

Nos 7005 *Lamphey Castle* of Worcester shed and 5042 *Winchester Castle* from Hereford grace the buffers at Paddington in 1954. The nobility of the locomotives influenced the men who worked them — or was it the other way round? *W. L. Kenning / Adrian Vaughan collection*

No 6004 *King George III* stands at Paddington in 1957, 'brewing-up' ready for the 'off'. Another of the mighty 'Kings' is arriving. *Adrian Vaughan collection*

No 6016 *King Edward V* with a Summer Saturday express from Paddington to Kingswear on 18 June 1960. The line ahead was crowded 'block and block', and 6016 was almost brought to a stand here, at Brewham Summit.
Hugh Ballantyne

Castle Cary Junction, looking towards Brewham Summit, in 1957, with No 5419 on an up stopping train waiting to leave.
Adrian Vaughan collection

the engine. In London during the war it used to get very thick, and on many occasions we would be very late bringing our engine off Old Oak due to the fog and frost. Tracking tender-first along the engine lines back to Paddington at 5mph, you could hardly see across the cab. One of the drivers I was with was Bill Hatch (another of the 'greats'), who knew the roads like the back of his hand: gradients, distances between signalboxes and signals, and how many signals there were per signalbox. In these dense fogs I would light the flare lamp, riding on the footstep at the far end of the tender and waving my mate on from there.

Out on the running lines, in fog, the ATC really came into its own. It was a wonderful thing that all GWR men were proud of. Of course, you still had to have your route knowledge to help you feel your way along *after* you'd been given an ATC warning. The driver had to know the sequence of signalboxes

A 'Hall' passes Athelney Junction with an up express. The right-hand signal arm routes from the down main to the Durston line — the original route of the Bristol & Exeter Railway from Yeovil to Taunton. The central arm takes trains down the 'cut-off' line, opened in April 1906. *Adrian Vaughan collection*

No 4978 *Westwood Hall* comes through Castle Cary Junction, at the foot of Brewham Bank, at 60mph, the maximum permitted speed for the reverse curves at the foot of the long, steep incline. *Peter Barlow Adrian Vaughan collection*

No 6025 *King Henry III* entering the final cutting before Whiteball Tunnel with the down 'Cornish Riviera' in the summer of 1951. The locomotive has a load of 10 coaches for around 355 tons, and has been climbing an average gradient of 1 in 86 for two miles and will have climbed lesser gradients for 5½ miles before that. At this point the train would have been running at about 45mph. In spite of the engine's great effort, there are no thick clouds of smoke — only a light grey mist and the 'white feather' at the safety valves. The 50sq ft of fire is white-hot, keeping the boiler at full pressure (250psi). There is no doubt this fireman is a master of his art, as was Bob Nicks. *Adrian Vaughan collection*

Overloaded with the 1.30 Paddington, No 6021 *King Richard II* is piloted by a 'Hall' as the train passes over Creech troughs in 1955. The carriage roofboards proclaim 'PADDINGTON, EXETER, PLYMOUTH AND PENZANCE'. *Kenneth Leech / Adrian Vaughan collection*

and the number of signals each 'box had. If you had a distant signal at 'Caution' you had to know whose distant signal it was and then how many stop signals it applied to — did this distant signal apply to one, two, or how many stop signals? If you thought there were two stop signals to look out for when in fact there were three, you would end up passing the third one at 'Danger' because you weren't looking out for it. Multiply that knowledge for the entire GWR main line from Penzance to Paddington (by two routes) and the roads to Shrewsbury and Swansea and you can appreciate what wonderful old boys those drivers were — their knowledge of the road was uncanny.

I well remember one night when I was booked out with George Highmore and 6018 for the 9 o'clock Penzance, midnight from Newton Abbot. The fog was dense and it was freezing too. Before I came off the shed I put oil on 6018's ATC shoe so that, if any water was splashed on it as we went over water troughs, it would not freeze up. I also had a bucket of dirty cleaning oil and cotton waste on the engine in case we needed to unfreeze our injectors.

We left Newton just after 1am in dense fog and were stopped a dozen times all the way up to London. After Reading the fog, together with some steam from around the engine, was so thick that we had a job to see across the footplate, never mind the end of the boiler. We were approaching Farnham Road signalbox, Slough, when we got the siren for its distant. Now you have to remember that these signals were lit by ordinary oil lamps; drivers had only the electric signals from Southall onwards — a help when finishing a long trip. My mate brought the train under control and crept along dead slow to find the home signal. Finally he stopped and said: 'Robert, I don't think we are very far from the signal.' I said I'd go out and look. I lit a flare lamp and walked along the footplating to the front end and we had stopped right in front of the signal which was at 'Danger'. What knowledge and judgement Driver Highmore had.

I also remember a trip up with the night Postal in 1946 with 5050 in fog and ice. I oiled the ATC shoe before we left. One of our injectors froze up at Swindon. While we were standing there I wrapped some 'oilies' round the injector body and, by setting them burning with the flare lamp, was able to unfreeze it. By the time we got to Paddington even the smokebox had a layer of frost, and the wheels and side rods looked a sight, with half an inch of white frost and icicles.

There was no doubt that some rough trips were made by the men working out of London or Bristol or South Wales. They saw some terrible bomb damage and destruction caused by fire when Jerry dropped his incendiaries. One of the most heartbreaking scenes from the Blitz was the hundreds of people accumulating every night in the Underground stations. You saw them on the

◄ A '47xx' 2-8-0 freight engine with a down express of 12 coaches has just left Whiteball Tunnel. Visible are Whiteball's down starting signals, with Burlescombe's distants below them. *Kenneth Leech / Adrian Vaughan collection*

Newton Abbot-based 'Castle' No 5073 *Blenheim* shows its superheater elements and inside steam pipes on Shrewsbury shed in 1957.
courtesy Russell Mulford

Shrewsbury shed yard in the 1950s, with No 5061 *Earl of Birkenhead* — aptly shedded at Chester — alongside Shrewsbury-based No 6980 *Llanrumney Hall.* A boy on the public footpath soaks up the atmosphere and, oblivious to the grime, dreams of one day being an engine driver. So many devoted railwaymen, including Bob Nicks, started off thus.
courtesy Russell Mulford

streets, carrying their bedding and a few possessions, to sleep as comfortably as they could, not knowing whether their homes would still be there in the morning.

Driver Jim Prowse and I were in the Victoria Palace for a show, second house, when an air raid was reported. I was one of many who did not like going into air-raid shelters because I felt that, if you were meant to die with a bomb, so be it, and I'd rather be out in the open than caught like a rat in a trap. All bus and Underground services were suspended, so we walked home to Wells House Road. Along the way we were stopped by police, air-raid wardens and the Home Guard and asked why we were out and not in shelters. We got back to the lodgings around a quarter to three next morning.

One night, lodging at 44 Wells House Road, there was just me and a chap from Laira in the house, apart from Hilda and her family, that is. About 2am Jerry dropped at landmine in the grounds of a factory behind our lodge, causing the house to rock and all the windows to be blown out. All the electric was gone so we got a torch and went downstairs, where Hilda was hiding under the stairs. We tried the gas, which was all right, and with the light of a couple of candles we made tea on the gas ring and waited for the raid to finish, which it did about 4.30am. When it got light we saw the place was a wreck, with all the windows gone, glass strewn over the floors downstairs and in the bedrooms, and plastered with soot and filth and brick-dust. It looked like a coalyard.

Still, despite all the difficulties, we chaps had some happy times.

The 'Cornish Riviera' in Cornwall. No 6915 *Mursley Hall*, in British Railways' 'mixed traffic' livery, runs into Bodmin Road station with the up express, blowing off steam whilst climbing a 1-in-65 gradient with eight ex-GWR coaches behind the tender. *courtesy S. C. Nash*

5. Driver at Last

No 6026 *King John* coasts towards its booked stop at Reading with the 1.30pm Paddington–Penzance. The train consists of 15 coaches; in those 'inefficient' coal-fired days, more coaches could be added to a train if passenger comfort required it. The distant signal for the Plymouth line, operated from Reading West main signalbox, can be seen about 10 coaches back. In the foreground is the 1896 connecting line to the Southern Railway. A permanent-way man and his imperturbable lookout pause in their work to admire the grandeur of locomotive and train. *Adrian Vaughan collection*

A Newton Abbot 'Castle' and its 'Devonian' crew heads for home out of Shrewsbury in 1954. *courtesy Russell Mulford*

I went into No 1 Link firing to Driver Highmore, who (as already demonstrated) was a master of route knowledge from Penzance to Shrewsbury or Paddington. As we went along he would ask me the sequence of 'boxes and how many signals each had. The work was nearly all booked work, and only three night jobs. These were the down Postal to Penzance and back, the 4.45pm Penzance–Bristol and a week at a time on the midnight — the 9pm Penzance, 1.20am Newton Abbot. Day work included the 'Torbay Express', (11.25am Kingswear–Paddington), the 8.45am Plymouth–Shrewsbury, some Bristol-and-back jobs with stopping trains, and one in the morning and one afternoon turn, all stations to Taunton. The work came easy with good mates because I had long been in training. Our engines on the Shrewsbury run were 5009 *Shrewsbury Castle*, 5011 *Tintagel Castle*, my favourite 5034 *Corfe Castle*, 5071 *Spitfire* and 5072 *Hurricane*. Now I was in

---

[8]. Bob had left the NUR and joined ASLEF when he became a fireman.

No 1 Link I was asked to become a Class Instructor, and I also became Assistant Branch Secretary of the Newton Abbot branch of ASLEF [8].

Driver Highmore was a man who enjoyed London and the races and football and a pint. He bet on a certain trainer's horses. His favourite dog track was Wembley. When we were off duty at Shrewsbury he used to take me out on the Severn in a boat, which he could handle well. His home was Marldon (near Paignton), where his father was the blacksmith, and they had a rowing boat on the beach at Paignton. Sometimes we would go to see Wolves play or visit Church Stretton, where there were some lovely walks on the Long Mynd overlooking Shrewsbury and the county of Shropshire.

I got to know the town park-keeper at Shrewsbury — Percy someone. He looked after the gardens of the park and the dingle by the river, marvellous flowers. I also went to the Shrewsbury Flower Show, which is world famous. We drank good beer in the

'Boar's Head', the 'Hen & Chickens' and the 'New Market House Vaults'. They'd have a great old sing-song in there on a Friday evening, and I sang 'You are my Sunshine' many times there. It was great enjoyment and a good laugh to be with George Highmore. He was a good mate.

George was thorough in his loco preparation and would help me find steam joints blowing and tell me to report them in the shed repair book — I learned a lot from him. He brought his grub to work wrapped in a white cloth in a wicker basket. The first time I fired to him I noticed he would open his basket to look in and then shut it again. I wondered what he was doing, and as we ran into Swindon at about 5.10am there was a great clanging and ringing from his basket — he had an alarm clock in there and he was checking our running times on it. I had two years with George and there was never an angry word. He finished when he was 63, just after I was passed for driving — thanks to him and men like him in the Newton Abbot Mutual Improvement Class.

Late in 1945 I had become the most senior fireman on the Great Western and so I went to Swindon for examination to be passed for driving. The Inspector at Swindon who conducted my examination on the locomotive and the Rules was Mr Lane, who had been a driver at Weston. After he had given me my driver's certificate I sent a wire to my mother at Kenton to give her the good news. I did not immediately take up driving duties but continued firing as a 'passed fireman'.

On the Saturday following, George Highmore and I were together on a Paignton and Plymouth turn, and that was his last day. We finished work about 2pm and we'd gone to the enginemen's cabin, where a lot of chaps wanted to say goodbye to him and wish him well. He went to a cupboard, got out a huge brown paper parcel and came back and said to me: 'Robert, you've been a good mate to me and you're the master of the job. So I must present you with a small token of remembrance.' He then handed me the parcel. I opened it and it was his flare lamp. He'd used it all the years when prepping an engine, and I used it all my time on steam. I still have it now, and it brings back wonderful memories.

At this time, link promotion for drivers at Newton was quite rapid, and two or three men were promoted to the Londons who had never worked over the road beyond Westbury or Bristol as firemen, but they signed for the road on account of the mileage pay they would get. They were rostered on the midnight turn, which is

From the footplate of a 'Castle' on a down express, the driver's view of the east end of Box Tunnel. Note the little tunnel and siding on the right; also the tidily maintained trees over the tunnel and the well kept grass. *Kenneth Leech / Adrian Vaughan collection*

41

A Newton Abbot-based
'Britannia', No 70022 *Tornado*,
stands alongside a 'Grange' as
the shed labourers discuss the
next job. With harsh conditions
like these to work in, all shed
staff and footplatemen *had* to be
of the most stalwart character.
The job demanded it — and
got it. As a result, the railway
with its steam engines was a
common-sense, reliable
organisation. *courtesy
Russell Mulford*

Stalwart men on Newton
Abbot shed in the 1950s:

L-R: Bill Bush, shed labourer,
Bob Nicks, the person above
Bob is unidentified, Shift
Foreman Fred Baker, Driver
Ern Carter, Shed Master Bill
Bearn, on the footplate of the
'WD', Fireman Ken Pretlove.
*courtesy Ken Pretlove /
Arthur King*

L-R: Fireman Ken Pretlove,
Bill Bearn, unknown, Bob
Nicks, Fred Baker, Ern Carter,
Fireman Ted Kavanagh.
*courtesy Ken Pretlove /
Arthur King*

more complicated because the signals look very different in the
dark from in daylight; these drivers asked me if I would go as their
fireman because their own firemen did not know the road either,
being No 2 Link men, so I was a good help to them. After George
Highmore retired I worked with Ern Ford, and he was glad to have
a chap with him who knew the road to Shrewsbury because he had
never been beyond Temple Meads either. I worked with Ern Ford
for about 10 weeks and was then appointed driver at Newton Abbot
in place of H. Leach, who had been off sick for nearly two years.
I worked my last firing turn to Paddington on the Sunday — the
2.40pm Paignton — and back with the 10.40 Paddington on the
Monday. I took up driving duties as from 2 February 1946. I got
handshakes from many drivers and firemen wishing me all the best,
as well as from Mr Sheppard and others of the management.

In 1946 we had 250 drivers and firemen on Newton Abbot shed.
It was a hive of industry, and from May to the end of summer
workings in October it was full-out: the shed itself and all the roads
were full of engines for weekend work, coalmen were loading
80 tons per shift and shed turners were kept busy on berthing and
pit duty. I started work on shed turning, yard shunting, banking

and assisting (being the pilot engine, coupled ahead of the train
engine), as well as 'Venlos'[9] to Kingswear to collect coal from
Renwick Wilton's coal boats and trains from there to Torquay or
Teignmouth, taking the coal to the gas works; I also worked
freight from Hackney Yard to Tavistock Junction, so altogether
I got good experience in handling both passenger trains and
freights over some difficult routes.

It was whilst in the Junior Link that I got into the only trouble
of my career. Twice when I was shed turning I got off the road —
both times with a '45xx' —because I didn't notice that the hand
points were not correctly set. On another occasion I got the blame
when the fusible plug on 5092 was found to be leaking, and I had
to go to see the Superintendent. I spoke to him like a man with
experience and got away with it — it was down to the Bristol
men, who had been running about with too little water in the
boiler. He told me to 'get out of the office'.

We handled locomotives of every class, including 'Kings',
'Castles' and '57xx'. In the Banking Link we had turns of eight
hours, working bankers from Aller Junction and Totnes, getting in

9. 'Venlo' was the codeword used in railway telegrams to indicate 'special empty
train running as under . . .'.

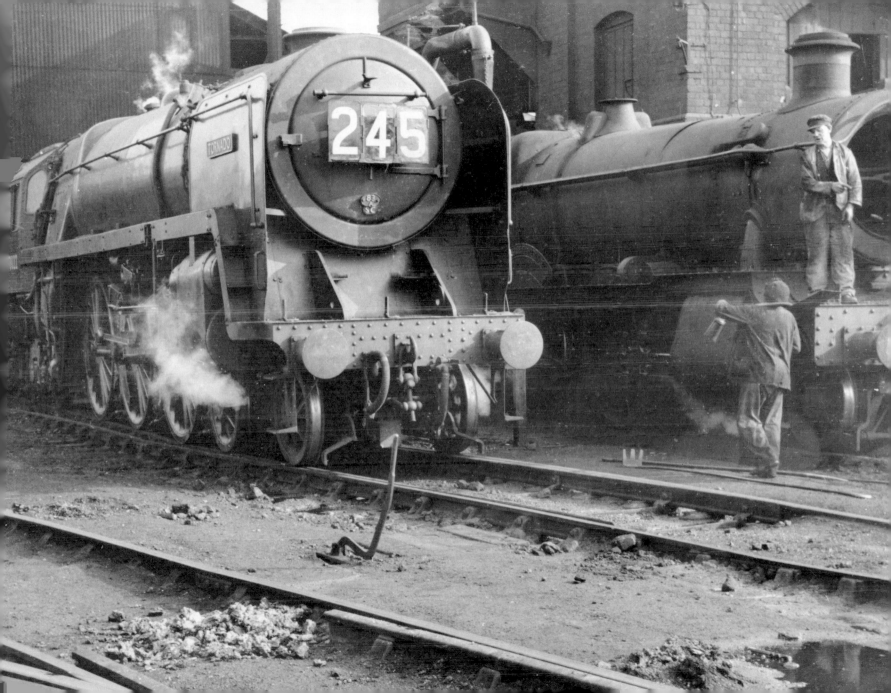

No 1011 *County of Chester*, near Teignmouth with the 11.20am Plymouth–Taunton stopping train on 2 August 1960. *Hugh Ballantyne*

Freight engine No 3862 brings a train of empty coaching stock under the Shaldon bridge towards Teignmouth on 2 August 1960. The headlamp over the right-hand buffer needs to be transferred to the left-hand to display the correct headcode. *Hugh Ballantyne*

◄ A Laira-based 'Castle', No 4098 *Kidwelly Castle*, gives assistance to a 'Warship' class diesel, No D602 *Bulldog* — overloaded for the South Devon banks — on the 6.25am Penzance–Paddington express, passing Brent, Junction for Kingsbridge, on Saturday 6 August 1960. *Hugh Ballantyne*

◄ At the heart of the railway was *coal*. Beautiful, Welsh steam coal. It glistened on the tender and burned in a white-hot fury. It was a truly stupendous sight to see. This is some of the supply for Laira shed. Nearest the camera is a 20-tonner, with mainly wooden wagons beyond that. Beyond, its fire looking like the sun and with steam blowing off at the safety valves, is a 'Grange' assisting a 'King' with an overload for the Devon banks. This is an 'Ocean Special' passing Laira Junction. The sights and sounds and the physical effort needed on that railway were at the heart of the morale that made it run so well. *Adrian Vaughan collection*

45

Bob Nicks would have passed under these signals thousands of times. Newton Abbot East 'box down starting signals, with West 'box distants. The East signalbox, opened in 1928, had a frame of levers numbered to 206. This was the scene in 1971. *Adrian Vaughan*

▲ eight or even 10 trips. I had some good firemen over the years: Claude Vosper, Arthur King and Ron Sharland were excellent at their work and as comrades. Eric Davey and I were together for nine years, working in the Shed Yard, Banking links and No 4 Link, Junior Main Line. He also liked to have a pint, but was very quiet and could always be trusted to get on with his work. He was a good driver too; I liked to fire, so we often changed sides. This gave both of us great pleasure, and we had great confidence in each other. Driving isn't so much a matter of 'going' as 'stopping'. You should manage the brake so you stop in one application, and the brake should be coming off as you stop so you have a 'cushion' stop and not a 'wheelbarrow' job.

There was one working where we used to work to Taunton and bring back the 4.20 Stoke Gifford–Hackney, and on this job we'd usually go into Victory Loop for a couple of hours — there were several down passenger trains and a parcels. First we'd go to the signalbox to find out how long we were likely to be detained, and then we'd tell the signalman where we were going and ask him to blow the engine whistle if he needed us sooner than he said, whereupon we'd come running; then Eric and I would go to a little

pub near Victory Crossing. Sometimes we'd have time for several pints before leaving, taking with us a bottle for the signalman.

There were some good signalmen around, like this man and those at Brent. When we went there to assist the 4.30pm Paddington or the parcels, which would be at Brent around 8.30pm or 9, they would put you in the branch bay out the way so you could go for a pint. When you were banking from Totnes the signalman at Rattery and Dainton would, on early turn, give you a chance to have a fry-up on the shovel — the finest meal there is.

In 1952 I was elected Secretary of the Local District Council on the union side, negotiating with the management. Although the old GWR company had disappeared, the work carried on much the same until 1958, when certain main-line rosters went over to being worked by D6xx 'Warship' diesels. We had a couple of these so as to teach our men this new type of traction — ours and Old Oak's were the first on the Western Region. With the coming of diesels there were continual redundancies at Newton Abbot, because they made it easier for management to parcel out the work to men at the far ends of the railway — Laira and Old Oak. The Beeching axe fell on all our branch lines, so Newton Abbot lost this work too.

No 6873 *Caradoc Grange* and a 'Castle' come storming down the 1-in-80 past Laira Junction signalbox. Ahead they have 1½ miles of level running before the start of Brunel's Hemerdon Bank — two miles at 1 in 42. The photograph was taken in 1960 by the signalman. *Larry Crosier*

Bob Nicks did not enjoy driving the 'Warships' — he was a steam man. Here is D814 *Dragon* with a Plymouth–Paddington express, signalled into the up main platform to stop at Reading in 1961. *Adrian Vaughan collection*

What a comedown! Bob Nicks at the controls of a diesel multiple-unit. Sadly, we do not have a photo of him on the footplate of one of his beloved 'Castles'. *courtesy Ivy Nicks*

When there were only 70 sets of men left on the shed we were forced to amalgamate the No 2 and No 1 links due to the loss of the Shrewsbury 'double home' work; we then worked only to Newport, whose men took the train on to Shrewsbury. We kept Paddington 'double home' turns, and it was at this time that the new hostel was opened at Old Oak, where the men were supplied with food as well as sleeping accommodation. Some of the men were very pleased; others weren't satisfied.

I was now driving in the main-line freight link, but the work was something of a shambles. There was less need for banking, with more powerful diesels and lighter goods trains, while coal trains were becoming fewer. The other depots were also trying to retain work, and Newton men found themselves covering shorter distances so other sheds could get a share of working the same trains. There were no trips to Penzance — only to Plymouth, Bristol and Westbury, mixed with spare turns where you just 'stood spare' awaiting a call from Control. Even the Senior Passenger Link had Penzance and Truro work only, plus spare turns. The bigger depots, such as Old Oak and Bristol, were now

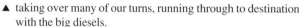

No 7001 *Sir James Milne* with an RCTS special on Brunel's great masterpiece, the Royal Albert Bridge, passing Saltash station's down home signal on 2 May 1959. Note the absence of trees growing out of the ironwork or the stone pillars supporting it. Morale and organisation were much better in 1959. *courtesy S. C. Nash*

taking over many of our turns, running through to destination with the big diesels.

In 1965 I went into the London Link as a senior driver. My turns in this link were not too bad, with a couple of weeks' work to London, a turn to Truro or Newport, another to Bristol and back and another to Westbury and back, plus spare turns, shared among 24 of us. I resigned as LDC Secretary the following year, by which time there were only 60 sets of men left at Newton Abbot. In 1968 all 'double home' working was abolished. The diesels were now rostered in a way that enabled management to shut out Newton Abbot and Exeter sheds altogether and to concentrate the work on Laira, Bristol and Old Oak. This caused another wave of redundancies, which saw a number of drivers back as second men. Also from 1968 the GWR system of link seniority was abolished, and the new entrant was on the same level as the top man. Under this new arrangement I found myself rostered on shed work and yard shunting, just as when I had first started driving, 25 years before. By 1969 Newton Abbot had only 33 drivers and 24 second men, with work to Bristol, St Austell and Westbury. The railway life was very flat and dull now, with redundancy everywhere.

On 8 January 1977 I decided to take redundancy under the Resettlement Agreement. I was the last of the 1929 cleaners.

My last working began at 10pm. Shed turning. I also had many weeks' leave due, which kept me on the paybill until the end of February 1977, giving me 47 years 7 months' service, during which I saw enormous changes. I don't know if they were for the best, but the pay was a lot better than it used to be. Talking of pay, in all my career I only once got a tip from a passenger — ten bob when we arrived at Paddington. I shared it half-and-half with my mate.

I was always very lucky to have a good wife who had worked in the gentry's service and knew how to keep the home running, cleaning and cooking, and we always had a good table. Believe me, this is one of the greatest assets to a footplateman. She and the children must often have wondered how I was getting on in London during the air raids.

During my footplate life I always tried to do my best and take an interest in my work, and to address all people in high office with respect and intelligence. I found this always paid dividends, as you were then known by your abilities and for being 'master of the job'. As a result I had no fear of the bosses, whatever their rank. The drivers to whom I fired would always defend a good mate, and I always admired the drivers I worked with — they were great stalwarts.

▲ Exeter St David's as Bob Nicks would have seen it as a teenager.
At the west end of the station, No 6018 *King Henry VI* stands gleaming
after a 173-mile run with the down 'Torbay Express' in October 1935.
A scene expressive of unity, competence and reliability.
D. R. Barber / Colour-Rail

49

▲ In spite of all wartime and early-postwar hardships, the GWR was still bravely maintaining near-perfection. No 5007 *Rougemont Castle* proudly enters Reading from the West in August 1947. Thousands of good men like Bob Nicks kept the flag flying through thick and thin. *H. N. James / Colour-Rail*

GWR enginemen attend to the needs of Churchward Mogul No 9303 on the down main at Reading station in April 1947. *H. N. James / Colour-Rail*

The honest reliability of 'Star' No 4061 *Glastonbury Abbey*, built by the Great Western for its own service, shines quietly forth under the skylights of Old Oak Common engine shed in September 1955 — much as Bob Nicks might have seen the engine 15 years earlier.
T. B. Owen / Colour-Rail

No 1466 stands at Moretonhampstead on a bright January day in 1959.
Peter W. Gray / Colour-Rail

Pannier tank No 3600 runs round its train in golden late-summer sunshine at Moretonhampstead in September 1958.
T. B. Owen/ Colour-Rail

▲ A 'Hall' heads down to Kingswear, crossing Broadsands Viaduct, between
Goodrington and Churston, on 13 September 1957. From up there, 100ft above the sea,
the lucky passengers — and the footplatemen — will have a glorious view of Tor Bay,
only 200yd or so from the railway. It was moments and places like this that made the
job worth doing. *W. Potter / Kidderminster Railway Museum*

▲ Churston, junction for Brixham, on 12 September 1957. Because all the trains were under the control of one authority, connections could be made between the branch train in the bay, hauled by No 1472, and the main-line trains. Nos 6814 *Enborne Grange* and 5178 wait with the very heavy Kingswear–Liverpool express while the Paddington–Kingswear, in the opposite platform, hauled by No 5008 *Raglan Castle*, drops passengers for Brixham. *W. Potter / Kidderminster Railway Museum*

▲ The fastest 'King' on the Western, No 6015 *King Richard III* (108½mph at Lavington early in 1957) running into Shrewsbury with an express from Paddington. No 7802 *Bradley Manor* is waiting to back onto the train to take it to Aberystwyth. Severn Bridge Junction signalbox was opened in 1903. It contained 180 LNWR signal and point levers and was 95ft long, the levers standing 24ft above the rails. The LNWR interlocking machine was clumsy and occupied two storeys. In 1952 a compact, GWR-type interlocking machine was installed for the same layout, making the lower locking room redundant. *Peter W. Gray / Colour-Rail*

Bob Nicks country. No 6004 *King George III* passes Dawlish down distant signal with a lightweight express in June 1958. When Bob saw the golden sands and red cliffs of Dawlish he knew he was nearly home. What a relief that must have been after a night under bombing in blacked-out London. *T. B. Owen / Colour-Rail* ▶

▲ No 1016 *County of Hants* gleams
on the engine line at Newton Abbot
West in August 1959.
Peter W. Gray / Colour-Rail

▲ No 4948 *Northwick Hall* standing on the engine lines at Newton Abbot West, waiting to take over train 113, a Paddington-Kingswear express, on 15 July 1959. The latter arrived behind No 5098. The 'Hall' is carrying Reporting No 535, which is the number of the train it will work back from Kingswear. *R. C. Riley*

59

▲ No 5065 *Newport Castle* has just arrived on Laira shed
from Plymouth North Road station after working in
with a train from Paddington on 17 June 1958.
W. Potter / Kidderminster Railway Museum

▲ Laira coaler, with No 7031 *Cromwell's Castle* buffered up
to a spanking tank engine, No 5567, on 17 June 1958.
W. Potter / Kidderminster Railway Museum

▲ No 5993 *Kirby Hall* draws forward off its train, the summer
Saturday 7.40am Paddington–Paignton. On the engine line a
string of locos and their crews await their duties.
R. C. Riley

▲ No 7824 *Iford Manor* runs in past Newton Abbot East 'box with a stopping train from Exeter on 15 July 1959.
R. C. Riley

▲ Working on the GWR or Western Region in steam days was, for the most part, like working in a beautiful garden, where hundreds of porters and platelayers, kept the route immaculate. No 1419 is seen on 4 July 1960 in the bay platform at Lostwithiel, waiting to take an idyllic mid-summer run down the wooded valley of the River Fowey to Fowey and on to St Blazey and Par. *W. Potter / Kidderminster Railway Museum*

▲ The flowers and the sparkling waters of the River Dart might cheer the spirits of the departing holidaymakers — or they might feel the worse for having to leave such a place. The enginemen could come here every day! No 5079 *Lysander* raises the echoes as it barks away up the valley from Kingswear with the 'Torbay Express' for Paddington on 23 June 1958.
W. Potter / Kidderminster Railway Museum

▲ The rail route from Newton Abbot to Shrewsbury passed through the 7,668yd (4.3-mile) Severn Tunnel. Bob would have passed through 'The Hole' thousands of times. Here, 'Britannia' No 70022 *Tornado* bursts out into the sunlight, blowing off steam after two miles' climbing a 1-in-100 gradient, with three miles of even steeper grades ahead.
P. M. Alexander/ Colour-Rail

Thanks to Mr Reg Hanks — an ex-Swindon Works apprentice — being Chairman of the Western Region, chocolate-and-cream coaches made a return to the best express trains. Mr Hanks also initiated the splendid headboards carried by the locomotives of named trains, and was unusual among top railway managers in that he loved firing express trains. Here, the result of his enthusiasm can be seen before and behind No 6017 *King Edward IV* as it surges away from Newton Abbot, unassisted for the Devon banks, with the 10.30am Paddington — the 'Cornish Riviera'. *L. F. Folkard / Colour-Rail* ▶

◄ No 1427 with its auto trailer at peaceful Ashburton station on 2 July 1957. *R. C. Riley*

▲ No 5536 awaits its next turn of duty at Exeter on 28 June 1957. *R. C. Riley*

▲ No 6908 *Downham Hall* scurries through the wide expanse of perfectly maintained and grass-free tracks at Laira Junction on 30 August 1961. *R. C. Riley / Kidderminster Railway Museum*

▲ The shed yard at Laira on 27 June 1960, with No 1011 *County of Chester* (far right), No 6972 *Beningborough Hall* (approaching), and the bunker end of a 'Superior 61xx', No 6166 under the shear legs. This device is used for lifting an engine, should a wheel spring or an axlebox require repair. *W. Potter / Kidderminster Railway Museum*

No 5934 *Kneller Hall* climbs the 1-in-80 gradient onto the embankment beyond Stoneycombe Cutting. Grades of 1 in 48 lie to the rear, while ahead lie stretches of 1 in 41 and 1 in 36, before the summit of the incline is reached inside Dainton Tunnel. It was on ferocious gradients such as these that Bob Nicks learned to fire. *Colour-Rail*

NBL 2,000hp 'Warship' diesel No D602 *Bulldog* crosses the dizzy heights of Largin Viaduct, 130ft above the valley. The view down would have been much more interesting from the doorless, semi-open cab of a steam engine, especially on a stormy day. In the background is Largin signalbox, a lonely place to work — a long, steep walk from anywhere, with the final approach across the windy viaduct. (See *Western Signalman*). *Colour-Rail*

▲ No 4978 *Westwood Hall* leaves Kingswear with a heavy load
of coal for Torquay gas works in June 1962.
Peter W. Gray / Colour-Rail

▲ No 7032 *Denbigh Castle* accelerates the 10.38 Saltash–Goodrington past Laira Junction on 30 August 1961; GWR ring arm signals on the left, GWR signal box, GWR goods brake van and vacuum-braked covered van — no diesel depot yet — everything as Bob Nicks knew it for 30 years, everything that worked well and was tried, tested and true. *R. C. Riley*

▲ Laira coaling stage, 27 June 1960. A hard-working coalman has heaved up the iron tram filled with ½ ton of coal, which can be seen pouring dustily into the bunker of the humble pannier tank. Meanwhile, on the left, No 6016 *King Edward V* and a 'Castle' are under disposal — fire cleaning and ash removal. *W. Potter / Kidderminster Railway Museum*

▲ No 6029 *King Edward VIII* cruises majestically out of Newton Abbot shed yard on 24 June 1960, passing one of the brand-new 'D63xx' diesels. The handsome looks and courageous challenge of the 'King' contrasts with the sullen boredom of the diesel. The former was good for men, the latter was not. *W. Potter / Kidderminster Railway Museum*

▲ Built in 1920 as an express goods engine and carrying out heavy express duties 40 years later, No 4704 stands at Newton Abbot with the 1.20pm Paddington–Kingswear on 15 July 1961. *R. C. Riley*

No D6305, a tolerably puny creature, presumes to assist No 5042 *Winchester Castle* out of Newton Abbot and over the Devon banks with the 12 noon Paddington–Plymouth express on 15 July 1961. *R. C. Riley* ►

Pewsey station, on the Berks & Hants Extension Railway, was opened in November 1862. Then merely a country branch line from Reading to Devizes, it was incorporated into an express main line to the west in July 1900 by the ever-vigorous Great Western Railway. Here, an ex-GWR flyer, No 5032 *Usk Castle,* saunters away towards Devizes with a local train in June 1962.
W. Potter / Kidderminster Railway Museum

No 6913 *Levens Hall* gallops through Maidenhead on the 'Silver Road' to Didcot. The 'Halls' were able to run at 80+mph on these long levels.
W. Potter / Kidderminster Railway Museum

▲ No 1007 *County of Brecknock* pulls way from Saltash station with the down 'Cornish Riviera' (10.30am Paddington), probably standing in for a failed 'Warship' diesel, in August 1959. *T. B. Owen/ Colour-Rail*

When trains were likely to be crowded, the steam-hauled railway could introduce extra trains without difficulty. Here, on 25 September 1960, No 5098 *Clifford Castle* hauls the 12.8pm Plymouth–Paddington — a 'relief' to the up 'Cornish Riviera' — past Lipson Junction, a mile or so east of Plymouth. The Penzance portion of the 'Riviera', the 'main train', left Plymouth at 12.20 hauled by D602 *Bulldog*, assisted by No 4950 *Patshull Hall. R. C. Riley*

No D847 *Strongbow* approaches Cowley Bridge Junction with the 12 noon Penzance–Manchester–Glasgow 'North Mail' on 5 July 1961. *R. C. Riley*

▲ The prototype '47xx', No 4700, at Newton Abbot on 4 July 1961, waiting to take its express train from London on to Plymouth. The '47xx' locomotives had eight driving wheels, of only 5ft 8in diameter, but were regularly used for West of England expresses when holiday-period schedules demanded 'all hands to the pump'. There were often occasions at Newton Abbot when four of them were together on the shed, having brought express trains down from Paddington or Bristol. They had two 19in-diameter cylinders (1in larger than standard) with a boiler pressure of 225psi. The fire-grate to be stoked by the fireman covered 30¼ sq ft, equal to that of a 'Castle'.
W. Potter / Kidderminster Railway Museum

▲ A glorious summer's day at Dulverton station, in rural Somerset. No 7304 on a Taunton–Barnstaple train is crossing No 6372 bound for Taunton while No 1421 stands at the branch platform with a connecting train to/from Tiverton. Is this the same planet we inhabit today? The important secondary main line that was the Barnstaple branch was strong enough to survive the first wave of Beeching madness but eventually succumbed on 3 October 1966. *Peter W. Gray/ Colour-Rail*

▲ Newton Abbot shed yard on 15 July 1961. A 'Hall' has the char removed from its smokebox while a '51xx' tank looks on. *R. C. Riley*

Engines waiting to go off shed, seen from Newton Abbot's down platform on a summer Saturday, 26 August 1961. *R. C. Riley* ▶

◄ No D6334 came on at Newton Abbot to assist
No 5008 *Raglan Castle* with the 12-coach,
12 noon Paddington–Plymouth express, seen
here climbing through Brent, junction for
Kingsbridge, on the way to Wrangaton Summit
on 26 September 1961. *R. C. Riley*

▲ Bob Nicks' favourite 'Castle' —
No 5034 *Corfe Castle* — standing under
the coaling stage at Bristol Bath Road
on 5 July 1959. Many enginemen
considered that the best 'Castles' were
those in the middle of the 50xx series.
R. C. Riley

No 4932 *Hatherton Hall*
passing Tiverton Junction with
a down 'H'-headcode freight
on 15 May 1962. *R. C. Riley*

▲ No 4993 *Dalton Hall,* having brought the 6.20pm Taunton into Exeter St David's on 23 June 1962, draws the empty coaches out onto the Exe bridge and reverses them to the up main to form a subsequent working. The GWR 'backing' signal on the bridge is cleared for the movement, passing the 131-lever West 'box. The latter can be enjoyed today in working order at Crewe Heritage Centre. *R. C. Riley*

▲ Dieselisation steadily removed jobs from Newton Abbot loco depot.
A Class 45 diesel roars up the 1-in-48 climb towards Stoneycombe
sidings with a down express in 1975. In the foreground is the reverse
aspect of a steam-age '50' warning drivers of a
'Permanent Restriction of Speed' for the 'S'-bend
through Stoneycombe. *Adrian Vaughan collection*

▲ North British-built Class 22 No D6334 pulls across the down main out of Stoneycombe Quarry to reach the up main with a load of ballast. Nowadays railway ballast is delivered by road. When the 'Link' system of promotion was abolished, Top Link men like Bob Nicks would have been rostered to such local trips as this, in between main-line express work. Note the good humour of the Newton Abbot men working this trip in putting up an express-train headcode — 1A47. By the time of the photograph — June 1971 — No D6334 was a Laira-based engine and one of the last of its type. It was withdrawn that October and scrapped the following April. *Adrian Vaughan collection*

A smart Class 253 High Speed
Train arrives at the western end
of the Western Region main
line under the control of
semaphore signalling. The
Class 253s took over the West
of England expresses from
1976. The service was faster
but often overcrowded,
due to the fixed formation
of only seven coaches.
Adrian Vaughan collection

In the new world created by modernisation, Bob Nicks found that redundancy was rife and reliability 'iffy'. All trains looked the same, and nothing was sacred; locomotives failed in charge of what had once been the most prestigious of trains — a phenomenon difficult for a steam-age railwayman to comprehend. Here, at Exeter St David's in the summer of 1980, the once famous and utterly reliable 'Cornish Riviera' is formed by a Class 253 which has broken down, and Class 50 No 50007 *Hercules* has come to the rescue.
Adrian Vaughan collection

Epilogue

Having left the railway, Bob took a job at a local school devoting his free time to his home and garden, and to the care of anyone in the vicinity of his home who needed it. He continued his love of sport and often went to London football matches on his railwayman's 'priv' ticket. He went up to Twickenham for a rugby international on 23 April 1991, getting home to Newton late. Next day he worked in his garden all morning. Ivy called him in to his lunch. He died suddenly, after his meal. His kindness and commitment to public service lives on in his children and grandchildren. His son is a schoolteacher, one grandson is a research biologist and the other a mathematician; his daughter maintains her mother's high standards of devotion to family.

Index of Locations Illustrated